BEING BRUJA

A Young Mystic's Guide

ZAYDA RIVERA

Illustrated by
JENNIFER DAHBURA

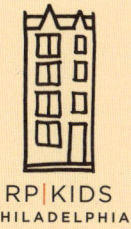

RP | KIDS
PHILADELPHIA

Text copyright © 2025 by Zayda Rivera
Interior and cover illustrations copyright © 2025 by Jennifer Dahbura
Cover copyright © 2025 by Hachette Book Group, Inc.

Running Press Kids
Hachette Book Group
1290 Avenue of the Americas, New York, NY 10104
www.runningpress.com/rpkids
@runningpresskids

Distributed in the United Kingdom by Hachette UK Ltd.,
Carmelite House, 50 Victoria Embankment, London, EC4Y 0DZ

First Edition: July 2025

Published by Running Press Kids, an imprint of Hachette Book Group, Inc.
The Running Press Kids name and logo are trademarks of Hachette Book Group, Inc.

The Hachette Speakers Bureau provides a wide range of authors for speaking events. To find out more, go to www.hachettespeakersbureau.com or email HachetteSpeakers@hbgusa.com.

Running Press books may be purchased in bulk for business, educational, or promotional use. For more information, please contact your local bookseller or the Hachette Book Group Special Markets Department at Special.Markets@hbgusa.com.

The publisher is not responsible for websites (or their content) that are not owned by the publisher.

Print book cover and interior design by Mary Boyer

Library of Congress Cataloging-in-Publication Data has been applied for.

ISBNs: 978-0-7624-8772-1 (hardcover); 978-0-7624-8773-8 (ebook)

Printed in Guangdong, China

1010

10 9 8 7 6 5 4 3 2 1

CONTENTS

❋

INTRODUCTION

A Letter to the Reader

❋

Have you ever thought of someone—maybe just for a second—and shortly after you see them walking down your block or they send you a text? Have you ever imagined yourself doing something really well, and when the time comes, it turns out exactly as you thought it would? Have you ever been able to feel someone else's feelings like they were your own?

If you answered yes to any of those questions: You. Are. Magic. It's time to embrace it—your inner bruja. Today, brujas, brujos, or brujxs (a gender-inclusive spelling) around the world are embracing what it means to *be* magic and to live freely and fully in that energy.

When you think of someone or imagine a situation and they appear or it comes true, it means you can manifest, or make your dreams and desires come to life. If you can do something that small, imagine what else you can create with your thoughts and intentions.

When you understand the importance of your breath, heartbeat, and connection to the Earth and your environment, you will feel where the magic begins. As you embrace your inner bruja and discover the ways in which you can live in full color and love, you will step into who you are and share your beautiful light with the world.

In this book, identifying as a bruja refers to the practice of working with the elements of life to which we are all connected. It is in no way about altering the will of another or taking control of things the Universe should handle. It is about understanding that we are truly cocreators of our lives with the Universe, and we can manifest anything if it aligns with our true essence and is based in love.

Are you ready? Let us begin.

Love,
Zayda

A Bruja's Beginnings

········ ✳ ·········

I remember the moment I started believing in magic. Not the magic that appears in movies and television shows with witches flying on broomsticks through the night sky and magical fairies with sparkly wands. Not that there's anything wrong with those fictional witches and fairies! I mean the true magic that comes from within us and goes beyond this human world.

At nine years old, I discovered that filling the pages of my journal with all the thoughts in my head brought me peace. One challenging day, I went to my room to be alone and write. Intuitively, or without thinking twice, I sat on my bed with my legs crossed in a meditation pose. Although I didn't know I was meditating at the time, I knew it was what I needed most in that moment. I closed my eyes and listened to my breath moving in and out of my body. Suddenly, I started to rock gently. I could physically feel myself moving. This wasn't the first time this happened to me. This gentle rocking had occurred a few times already, in moments when I needed to get away and sit alone in my bedroom with my eyes closed, listening to my breath. I enjoyed the feeling and was curious to discover more.

The first few times, I was too nervous to open my eyes, but that day I wanted to. I slowly opened my right eye and then my left eye as I looked down at my lap, still feeling the rocking, and I could see my body moving ever so slightly. It was such a small movement that if I didn't also feel it, I may not have been able to see it happening. But it was! Something that made me feel safe was present in those moments when I needed comfort, peace, and protection.

What surprised me most was that I wasn't scared. I knew that it was something good and that the second I welcomed it, it would be present in my life forever. Whatever the source was, it transformed how I thought about the world from that moment on. I knew something greater than myself was looking out for me.

As I continued to explore that "something greater," I navigated different religions, attending a variety of church services with family members—Catholic with my maternal grandmother, Baptist with my aunt, and Pentecostal with my parents and siblings. I found beauty within the different houses of worship, but not the deeply authentic connection that I felt sitting quietly on my bed, listening to my breath. I wanted to discover more of what that was and the role it played in my life.

The ways in which I have chosen to communicate with the Higher Power, my spirit team (more on that later), and the elements—earth, water, air, fire—have caused some to label me a bruja, a term that has been widely misunderstood throughout history and to this day. While we are currently witnessing an acceptance of the word, there are still so many people who misunderstand what being a bruja truly means. Whether you decide to embrace it, acknowledge it, or reject it altogether, it's important to know and understand the roots of the term and its journey so you can choose whether it is something that you'd like to explore in your life.

CHAPTER ONE

BRUJA: AN EXPLORATION OF THE WORD

What Does Bruja Mean?

.... ✳ ....

It's amazing how one word can hold so much meaning and history, so many emotions and stories. Bruja is a powerful declaration. Its origin is hard to pin down, but the word bruja is international and cross-cultural.

For centuries, bruja, which is Spanish for "witch," has been used around the world and defined in many ways, depending on the situation for which it was used. Typically, the word bruja has been associated with Latin American mysticism. From the Caribbean to Mexico and the far reaches of Central and South America, brujxs have existed.

While the meaning of the word continues to evolve, past taboos around what brujería means (and what brujas do) impact how it is viewed today. In the past, and still to this day (though increasingly less often), brujas have been portrayed as something bad or evil.

We've all seen the story of the good witch and the bad witch. From movies like *The Wizard of Oz* or *Halloweentown* to shows like *Sabrina the Teenage Witch* and *Wizards of Waverly Place*, along with recently released movies like *Hocus Pocus 2*, the image of a scary-looking woman with a pointy hat flying around on a broomstick is one we know. While this is for entertainment purposes, the way brujas are shown in what we watch, from how they dress to how they live, influences the way society looks at brujas.

History of Brujería:
From Origins to Conquistadors

···········❖············

H istorically, brujas were important members of society, providing healing to those in the community. In many parts of the world where brujería has been practiced, it was also used in celebrations of marriage, birth, and even death. The mysticism of the craft came from working with earthly companions like herbs, flowers, plants, and sacred trees, as well as the elements of water, fire, and air. Brujas understood the power of working with the flow of the moon's phases, as they can impact and transform life.

Brujas prepared sacred baños and limpias (the Spanish words for spiritual baths and cleansings) using herbs, oils, flowers, and other essential ingredients to help heal trauma or cleanse negativity and stagnant energy to create space for manifestations. We'll dive deeper into these sacred rituals in later chapters.

Depending on the geographic location, they went by different names. In Mesoamerican traditions—which were found in parts of Mexico and Central American countries like Guatemala, Honduras, Belize, El Salvador, Nicaragua, and Costa Rica—these healers were referred to as curanderas, curanderos, and shamans, names that are still used today.

The Indigenous people of the Caribbean are the Taínos. They referred to their medicine people or healers as behikes. These were essentially the doctors of the villages and if you were sick mentally, physically, or spiritually, you would visit the behike. Depending on what ailment you faced, the healer would decide upon what ritual needed to take place to begin the healing. It could be a ritual cleansing using the four elements and include music, singing, dancing, and chanting, or it could simply be a special tea to drink. Whatever the case was, the goal was to heal and overcome the ailment.

These healers were also important parts of community rituals and celebrations, often leading the village in prayers, or invocations of Spirit, Source, God, or the Universe, which all refer to the same thing—the acknowledgment of a Higher Power assisting us and guiding us on our human journey.

Some Indigenous groups regarded those Higher Powers as a variety of gods who were responsible for different things in our lives. For example, santería, the religious tradition of African origin found primarily in Cuba and parts of the Caribbean, acknowledges several gods or deities, like Yemaya, the queen of the sea, or Oshun, an important river deity.

In the 1400s, when European explorers set sail to different parts of the world, they met with civilizations that had existed for thousands of years prior to their arrival, including the Taíno of the Caribbean, who were the first people Christopher Columbus met when his ship reached land in 1492. Within these societies, brujería and other forms of Indigenous spiritual beliefs and religions were practiced and deemed by the explorers as evil simply because they didn't understand them, and it differed from what they practiced—a widely embraced religion in Europe called Christianity.

The explorers would infringe upon these lands inhabited by Indigenous groups, learn their ways of life, and go back to Europe to share stories of exploration and findings, only to then return to those foreign lands once again and implement, often by force, their own traditions largely based around the Christian faith. This quickly altered the meaning and views around the community healers—or brujas, curanderas, or behikes—as practicing traditions that were against the Christian way and in turn considered evil, blasphemous, or sacrilegious. If the villagers denied embracing the explorers' faith, they would face consequences that included slavery, poverty, and even death.

Keeping Brujería Alive

Despite the efforts of the conquistadors, Indigenous spiritual practices continued, often carried out under the moonlight away from the watchful eyes of the colonizers. These nighttime rituals were used by the newcomers as examples to further stake their claim that the

Indigenous spiritual practices were based on dark magic and so needed to be practiced away from daylight—a narrative that continues as a stereotype today.

As Christianity became the dominant religion practiced around the world, Indigenous spiritual practices fell further into the shadows. The consequences were great for those who continued practicing spiritual rituals outside of the Christian faith, causing many people to convert and disconnect from ancestral Indigenous wisdom. Others continued practicing privately, incorporating Indigenous rituals at home while devoting themselves to the church in public.

It's important to note that over generations people from the Indigenous lineages deeply embraced Christianity, and it is evident today with their descendants. Many Latine families are devout churchgoers, and still, those Indigenous spiritual practices live on in their faith.

THE SIGNIFICANCE OF HEAD WRAPS

People who continued to practice Indigenous spiritual rituals would sometimes wear items symbolic of their faith. The head wrap was one way to honor those practices without the colonizers knowing what it symbolized. This piece of fabric wrapped around the head represented history, spirituality, and resistance to the oppression Indigenous and enslaved people were experiencing.

The head wrap journeyed from Africa to the Caribbean and Latin America, influencing spiritual and cultural traditions by way of the transatlantic slave trade and across the African diaspora, which scattered, displaced, and forced people from one place to live in separate communities. During that journey, the head wrap defined many things like protection from the hot sun while working in the fields for several hours, as well as spiritual protection. It also served as a cover-up to the intricate escape routes slaves took to freedom. The routes were interwoven in their hairstyles with braids and twists, and the head wraps hid these maps to freedom.

The powerful symbolism of the head wrap is also evident with the misa, a spiritual gathering practiced in santería and within the African diasporic religion candomblé, practiced in Brazil. Settlers tried to change the way head wraps were used through efforts like the tignon laws of Louisiana in the 1700s, which forced freed African women to wear a headscarf to cover up their culturally significant and often elaborate hairstyles and distinguish them from the wealthier class.

Despite their efforts, head wraps continued being used as spiritual symbolism, which is still evident today. As a form of resistance, the Indigenous and enslaved people began wearing the most fabulous head wraps. Instead of just being a piece of fabric wrapped around the head, it became a fashion statement with jewels and feathers and beads.

Today, many spiritual practitioners wear head wraps to honor how our ancestors wore them both as a fashion statement and for spiritual rituals and ceremonies. The belief that the head wrap protects the crown chakra and the movement of energy, which travels up the spine and out of the top of the head or crown, is still relevant in spiritual practices today.

CHAPTER TWO
BRUJXS IN
THE WORLD TODAY

The "Good" and the "Bad"

························❋·······················

Nearly everything in life has a good and a not-so-good side to it. Brujería is no different. "Black magic" stereotypically refers to spells, and other ritual work, that involve controlling someone else's willpower, changing someone else's circumstances without their consent, and work that is generally considered evil. On the flip side, spiritual work that focuses on cleansing the spirit, easing anxiety and stress, and removing negative and stagnant energy to create space for manifesting may be defined as "white magic." The contrast between black and white magic is influenced by history and pop culture, which continues to imply the outdated and wrong idea that anything black is bad and white is good. For the purposes of this book, we strike out the use of the terms black and white magic and focus on positive, loving spiritual work centered on healing and finding balance, and not work intended to harm people, places, and things.

Of course, there are some who use the practice of brujería in bad ways. This may include casting spells or hexes on others to change the course of events or an outcome to a situation. This book is not at all about those kinds of practices.

When you use your inherent magic to send negative energy to another individual, you do more harm to yourself than you do to them. Even more, if you try to work with magic intended to control or hurt someone else, you are instead blocking your own path to greatness. So lead with love, intend to heal what needs to be healed, and open your heart to the immense beauty this life can bring if you are willing to see it, believe in it, and receive it. The magic you will learn about in this book will focus on love, healing, shadow work, and creating space for growth and transformation.

Posers versus Longtime Students of the Craft

As you seek knowledge and quench your thirst for a deeper understanding of magic, you will come across various teachers. Choosing the right ones could be the biggest intuition test of your life. Don't believe everything you hear on social media and the internet. Remember that those platforms are free and open to anyone who wants to use them. And just like the good and the not-so-good magic we previously discussed, not everyone talking about brujería or spirituality online has the best intentions.

There are a few things to consider when looking for reputable spiritual teachers. Find out where and why they learned how to do the work. Was it passed on through generations of spiritual practitioners or brujas in their family, or did they study with credible teachers? Seek out longtime students of the craft, whether it was a part of their family or acquired through disciplined study. Steer clear of those who jump on the trends train. Following spiritual practitioner posers could lead to receiving false information that further perpetuates stereotypes and myths about what it means to be a bruja.

How Is Bruja Used Today?

As brujería grows in popularity on social media, more people are using it as a source of empowerment and freedom from societal constraints. A bruja is often an independent thinker who learns to work with the elements to create magic in their life and in the lives of others. Anyone, regardless of gender identity, can deem themselves a bruja. If your preference is brujo or brujx—that's great! No one decides but you. In this book the terms are used interchangeably because magic exists in all of us regardless of gender. These practices typically take place outside of religion and are focused instead on embracing spirituality. These days anyone can be a brujx, including your friends or colleagues living in big cities and the suburbs.

In many Latine households today you can find religion and spirituality crossing paths. There may be acknowledgment, understanding, and beliefs around a specific religion while also finding importance in Indigenous spiritual wisdom, which some may refer to as brujería.

As someone who has practiced spirituality and Indigenous spiritual traditions for over a decade, what I realized as an adult is that my devout Catholic grandmother was also faithful to ancestral practices. While Catholicism was something of great importance in her life, she would also do simple practices rooted in Indigenous spiritual traditions like placing bowls of water throughout her house to absorb negative energy or redecorating all the rooms in her home with the changing of the seasons to refresh the energy and keep blessings and abundance flowing freely. I never heard her utter the words bruja or brujería, and I didn't know anything about it as a child, but I understood that religion and spirituality could be practiced at the same time. Although she didn't identify with the word bruja, her actions embraced the spiritual traditions carried on from her ancestors and mine.

Being bruja means awakening the light within us. It's like having a conversation with the Universe that helps guide us on our human journey. It's a frequency. A vibration. There's a certain internal rhythm to it. Understanding that magic within you is one thing. Knowing, feeling, and seeing it play out in your own life is how you truly embrace the word bruja and celebrate it within yourself. Once you discover how connected you are to everything around you, your life will never be the same again.

CHAPTER THREE
EMBRACING YOUR INNER BRUJA, SPIRIT, AND NATURE

The beautiful thing about awakening to Spirit is that once it begins, there is no stopping it. I like to think of it as a light switch that turns on and off at different times in our lives. For me, the light switch flipped on for the first time in my life at nine years old. But it didn't stay fully on. That light dimmed greatly as I was growing up and navigating middle school, high school, and even college. It wasn't until I graduated from college and decided to move to Hawaii on a whim that I saw the light again.

The first day I landed in Hawaii, I was excited yet nervous to be so far away from my family for the first time in my young life, especially my mom. I sat on my hotel bed and cried as I questioned my decision to pack up my life and move. Then, I felt a little nudge, like someone was telling me to pick my head up and look out the window. When I looked out at that spectacular ocean view, a beautiful rainbow appeared. I don't know how long I sat there staring at that rainbow, but I knew it was a message from something so much greater than myself that everything would be okay. This was the new start of my journey, and while I would face uncertainty and fear again, I could feel confident that I would never be alone.

Remember: that light may dim and brighten at different times along your journey, but once it's illuminated, once you begin believing in the magic within you and your connection to everything, that light will never go dark again. It may dim so much that you can barely see or feel it, but it's there. Trust in it.

What Is a Spiritual Awakening?

............✽............

Spiritual awakening begins when you first connect to your soul and realize there is a deep consciousness that you can tap into for guidance, protection, love, healing, and peace. It's up to you whether you want to continue diving deep into the infinite possibilities that come from that awareness.

You can experience a spiritual awakening more than once in your life. Remember the light switch? Once it turns on it will never fully go dark again. At times your light may dim to the lowest level, making it hard to see it. Along your journey, your wisdom will help you become more comfortable listening to the messages you receive from your own consciousness, the Universe or Higher Power, and your spirit team, which includes ancestors or people from your family that have passed on, as well as other energies intended to protect and guide you on your journey, such as animal spirits and angels. Whenever you find yourself feeling lost in life, or feeling like anxiety is getting the best of you, you can tap into your spirit team to support you. We each have a team supporting us, waiting for us to ask for help. The act of asking shows that you believe there is life beyond the physical and you are open to working with it.

How to Connect with Spirit

The word "Spirit" in this book refers to our true essence as well as a Higher Power helping to guide and cocreate our lives. There are several variations of the term. Some may call this Higher Power or energy, God, Source, or the Universe, and some Indigenous communities refer to it as the Great Mystery. It's more of a feeling. A deep knowing that we are not alone.

Whether you're going through a difficult time or you're experiencing pure elation, Spirit is there. Spirit exists within us and in everything around us. Spirit can be found in the petals of a flower, the wings of a honeybee, the raindrops that fall upon the earth, the depths of our vast oceans, rivers, and lakes, and in the moon and stars. So connecting to Spirit is as simple as becoming aware of your surroundings and acknowledging that you are energy that is flowing with all the energy around you found in the four elements and everything in existence.

Nature Connections

✻ · · · · · · · · · · · ✻ · · · · · · · · · · ·

BEING OF THE LAND

For generations, Indigenous people have believed that there is no separation between the land and us. We are one and the same. Our planet reflects us, and we are a reflection of it. One of the biggest ways to show this reflection is through water, which makes up more than half of our planet, as well as ourselves. Just as the tides rise and fall with the moon phases, we, too, are impacted greatly by the cycles of our lunar companion. The same can be said about the rising and setting of the sun. This is why working with the moon and sun has always been such a staple in Indigenous spiritual practices.

Think about the seasons. As we embark on the winter season, many people start to feel the call to slow down, go within, and embrace more stillness. Our animal friends feel the same, which is why we see so many of them hibernate through the winter months, rising again as the flowers bloom in the spring. This is why Indigenous spiritual practices include herbs, plants, flowers, and other earthly elements. There is a direct connection between the cycles of our earthly companions and us. This connection is deeply felt if you allow yourself to feel it. The best way to do so is simply believing that we are connected to the trees we pass by every day, the flowers we marvel at, and the earth we move upon.

Give it a try yourself. See and feel the powerful connection between us and a beautiful flower by sitting with it and staring at its beauty. Really allow yourself to see the flower beyond its surface. The petals, the stem, the leaves, the roots. It is truly a miracle how this flower grows from seed to full blossom. Stare at the petals, and if you want to, set the intention to receive messages from the flower. What you hear may surprise you. Some Indigenous beliefs hold that flowers have a soul and can even be an ancestor reincarnated. The same can be said of birds and any living thing.

Staring at a flower is one way to connect. You could also connect through meditation, prayer, singing, eating mindfully, and maintaining your spiritual wellness by including daily practices intended to uplift and awaken your soul.

UNDERSTANDING THE FOUR CORNERS

Working with the elements of earth, air, fire, and water means you acknowledge the connection we have with the world, everything in it, and the magic within you that aligns with a universal life force energy. Think of it as a pulse or a beat that we are in constant rhythm with as long as we work daily with things like feeling grateful, not worrying, not allowing anger to overcome us, and treating others with kindness. We may not always get it right, and feelings of being off-balance indicate we're slightly off beat with that life force energy. The good news is, we have the strength to get back on rhythm through breathwork, meditation, prayer, and other spiritual rituals like limpias or cleansings and baños or sacred spiritual baths (more on baños and limpias in chapter ten).

One way to converse with the Universe and show gratitude for that powerful connection is to call on the four corners at the start of spiritual rituals. The four corners generally represent the four cardinal point directions—north, east, south, and west—but are also aligned with the four elements—air (north), earth (east), fire (south), and water (west)—and colors representing the sun moving across the sky. White is the light of dawn representing the east, the blue sky of daytime is the south, the yellow evening sunset is the west, and the black of the night sky represents the north. Our ancestors would use the points or corners to help direct them as they navigated the land, but they also used them as a resource for aid in spiritual healing.

Each direction symbolizes something different within us, which is another way of acknowledging the sacred connection between our energy and the Universe. Indigenous spiritual wisdom also defines the four directions or four corners within the stages of life, the seasons of the year, and the aspects of life. There are four stages of life with birth, childhood, adulthood, and death, as well as four seasons of the year—winter, spring, summer, and fall. The aspects of life are all the layers of ourselves that need love, and becoming aware of all four—physical, mental, emotional, and spiritual—and how we flow through life when they are in balance ensures a magical existence. The four corners sometimes refer to animal spirits as well. The Taínos believed sacred birds represented the four directions.

ANIMAL GUIDES

Hummingbirds symbolized the north and represented all the wisdom we gain through life experiences. The mighty hawk represented the east and a confirmation that when we live in balance with the Universe and remain present, our lives will be bright and beautiful. The turkey symbolized the south, our innocence, and being open-minded, and the wise owl represented the west, the direction that inspires us to dive deeply within ourselves to find the answers to our questions about life, as it is associated with our shadows and the night.

In curanderismo, it is believed that pieces of our soul may journey away from us depending on what we experience in life. We can retrieve those soul pieces by working with the different corners, or cardinal directions or spaces. In the south, we begin our journey of soul retrieval by discovering and understanding what occurred that sent that piece of our soul on a journey, and how to bring it back home. In the west, we focus on releasing what no longer serves us, like bad habits, and on rediscovering our strength. The north is where the guidance of our ancestors lives. Their wisdom helps to light our path if we are willing to listen. Once we discover the source of the problem or challenge we face (south), work to release the tension, anxiety, or stress it causes (west), and tune into the guidance from our ancestors (north), we have created space for new beginnings, which exist in the east.

Brujas, curanderas, shamans, behikes, witches, or whatever you wish to call spiritual practitioners or spiritualists, all work closely with the four directions and the symbolisms and representations associated with each. Setting the intention to work with the four corners is easy. Simply acknowledge each space by standing and facing the south, then turning to face the next direction, and then the next until you've saluted all four. You can use a spiritual tool as you do this to have a more physical representation of what you are invoking spiritually. Some spiritualists use a conch shell and blow into it, making a loud horn-blowing sound in each direction. Others may use smoke by burning sage or palo santo to represent the element of air.

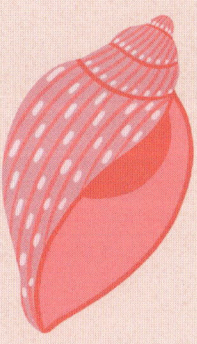

The sacred smoke is then either blown or fanned with a feather in the direction you are facing. This is performed by experienced spiritualists and is not recommended for beginners. If you're curious about smoke, do not do so without the supervision of an adult. Sometimes the intention is said verbally to acknowledge the four corners, or an altar can be created with a variety of materials, some of which point in the four directions. Even if you have none of these items to work with, you can simply tap into your heart and face each direction, giving pause as you turn from one corner to the next, acknowledging and showing gratitude for what the four corners represent in our lives.

Get creative. What calls to you? More important than anything else, when tapping into the magic within, use your intuition. What is that inner voice telling you? Listen closely and don't second-guess it. As your practice deepens, so will the ability to hear your intuitive voice, and you will begin hearing the difference between that guidance and the ego voice blocking your path with anxiety, worry, self-doubt, negativity, and procrastination.

CHAPTER FOUR

ESSENTIAL ELEMENTS

Putting Your
Brujería into Practice

· · · · · · · · · · · ❋ · · · · · · · · · · · ·

The four elements should be represented in your spiritual practices. There is also a fifth element to consider, and that is you. Your intuition and intention around your practices are key ingredients, always. They are the fire that ignites your magic. You are the air that flows with the Universe to create beautiful things. Your physical body can represent water, the element it is primarily made of, and you are one with the earth. The elements exist within you. So think of the other tools and ingredients you'll use in your magical practices as the icing on the cake, and you are the cake. The magic begins within you!

Candles

· · · · · · · · · · ✳ · · · · · · · · · ·

Candles are a wonderful item to include in your spiritual practices to represent the fire element. The color of the candle symbolizes different things like the corresponding zodiac sign, chakras, and various intentions. For example, a black candle may be used for protection, and a pink candle can be used for self-love. A green candle can correspond to the heart chakra, which is represented by the same color.

RED	Love, stability, grounding (associated with the root chakra)
ORANGE	Creativity and our identity (associated with the sacral chakra)
YELLOW	Confidence, clarity (associated with the solar plexus chakra)
GREEN	Money, abundance, love (associated with the heart chakra)
BLUE	Expression, wisdom, spirituality (associated with the throat chakra)
INDIGO	Self-reflection, knowledge (associated with the third eye chakra)
PURPLE	Intuition, wisdom (associated with the crown chakra)
GOLD	Success, abundance (associated with the crown chakra)
WHITE	Healing, protection (associated with the crown chakra)
PINK	Self-love, friendship
BLACK	Protection
BROWN	Balance, stability
GRAY	Protection, neutralizing

Whenever you use an open flame in your rituals, use caution and get an adult's help. Pray and set your intentions before lighting the candle. The flame represents your intention in physical form. As it burns, your intentions are illuminated. You can even carve a word or symbol in the wax prior to lighting the wick or bless it with an herb bundle that coincides with your intention. Bay leaves have been used to set intentions around abundance. You can take some bay leaves and place them around the candle holder before lighting the candle. Take a step further and write your intentions on the bay leaves with a pen or marker. The flame from the candle symbolizes your intentions being sent into the ether.

Palo Santo

❖

Representing both the earth and air elements is palo santo. The air element comes from the smoke that dances off the holy wood when it is burned. This sacred tree has been used as a powerful cleansing tool during spiritual practices since the Inca Empire. Shamans and healers from

South America believed the trees should never be cut down and should not be used for spiritual rituals or ceremonies until four to ten years after they have naturally fallen to the forest floor. According to tradition, the tree's spirit continues to live in the wood after death, and if treated properly during its lifetime, that strong spirit will assist in the restoration of physical and energetic well-being.

Burning palo santo, sage, or other spiritual healing herbs, woods, and resins is for advanced spiritualists. Instead, you can use a spray or essential oils in a diffuser to bless the space without burning anything. Make sure you have adult supervision.

Sage and Other Spiritual Cleansers

· · · · · · · · · · · ❋ · · · · · · · · · · ·

This sacred herb has been used in spiritual practices for centuries, typically by Indigenous peoples from the southwestern region of the United States as well as parts of Mexico. In curanderismo, sage is widely used for limpias or energy cleansing with its purifying smoke. But sage is not the only herb traditionally used for this purpose. It has become a bit of a pop culture icon thanks to its purifying smoke, but Indigenous communities around the world have long used other herbs and resins with the same intention of clearing negative, stagnant, and evil energy.

Copal is a tree resin that was used in pre-Columbian Mesoamerica, which includes parts of Mexico and Central America as well as the Andean region of western South America. This included the Mayans and Aztecs, who called copal resin "the blood of trees" and used it in spiritual ceremonies and rituals to cleanse and purify in a similar way to how sage is used. Copal also served the purpose of honoring deities and ancestors during ceremonies and rituals. It has also been found to be a powerful pairing with meditation and manifestation. The smell is distinctive and quite calming, filling the air with the sweet aroma of pine and earth. While it's grounding, it also allows your soul to set sail. Other herbs and resins that create purifying smoke include sweetgrass, juniper, and cedar.

The Taínos, or the Indigenous peoples of the Caribbean, used the resin from another sacred tree called tabonuco to cleanse impurities from a person inside and out. This smoke is believed to be a tool for prayer and communication with the other realm, and it was intentionally used to cleanse entities the Taínos called maboyas, or all the unclean obstructions in our path. It was used when a person was sick, or even when they were filled with resentment and anger.

Tobacco is indigenous to North and South America. It is derived from the leaves of the genus *Nicotiana* plant. It is considered a part of the nightshade family of plants, which also includes tomatoes, eggplant, potatoes, and peppers.

In shamanic practices, tobacco smoke is used for healing and blessings, and it can also be an offering to the spirit world. While it was smoked during some spiritual rituals, it was also used for smudging or cleansing spaces by burning the dried tobacco leaves. It is believed to be a soul-opening plant that removes negative energy and elevates healing powers. Another form of tobacco used in spiritual rituals comes from the Amazon and is called rapé. This dried, powdered snuff tobacco is used as a powerful tool in healing practices. The tobacco used for healings and blessings is not like the tobacco used for cigarettes. Tobacco is most widely known as containing nicotine, which is a highly addictive chemical often found in cigarettes. In the past century, we've learned a lot about how bad smoking cigarettes or tobacco of any kind is for your body, and they should not be used for any sort of cleansing, spiritual or otherwise.

Salt

Salt isn't just for seasoning food. This powerful mineral has been used in Indigenous spiritual practices for generations, representing purification and a connection to the earth. When in its purest form, not iodized or table salt, it can help the body and spirit heal by cleansing us physically and energetically. Epsom salt, sea salt, and pink Himalayan salt are commonly used for cleansing baths. Salt lamps are also popular. The salt is believed to extract or release toxins like negative energy that may be causing fatigue and illness.

Indigenous spiritual practices included the use of salt for protection of the home, sacred spaces, and ourselves. It can help repel evil spirits and absorb negative energy from a physical space or our aura, the electromagnetic energy field that surrounds or encompasses the physical body.

Pink Himalayan salt is over 250 million years old and has been used for centuries in shamanic spiritual traditions for purification and the removal of stagnant and negative energy. It is considered the purest form of salt and contains all eighty-four natural minerals found in the human body.

Sea salt is another popular salt to use. For centuries, it has been hailed for its spiritual benefits because it's loaded with minerals and can detoxify the spirit body as well as the physical body from ailments like skin conditions while also easing aches and pains.

Salt has been used widely in spiritual practices for the removal of toxins and negativity. It can also be included for its restorative properties. It is an important ingredient in spiritual baños and limpias. By soaking feet or hands in warm water mixed with salt, flowers, and herbs, a person can restore their spiritual health and overall balance.

Agua de Florida (Florida Water)

· · · · · · · · · · · ❊ · · · · · · · · · · · ·

Agua de Florida, or Florida Water, is a spiritual cologne that has been used in spiritual practices around the world. In curanderismo, Florida Water is used often for cleansing, protecting, and restoring the mind, body, and spirit. It is also great for cleansing spaces.

It contains alcohol as its base combined with flowers, herbs, and spices. Adding Florida Water to your spiritual baño or limpia is believed to elevate its magical properties. It's great for cleansing negative and stagnant energy from your home, yourself, someone else, or an object. Do this by using a spray bottle to spritz your room or around yourself before you head out for the day.

You can also spray it on your palms and wipe your body down after a long day to remove outside energy. It can even help bring good vibes to a sticky situation and has been found to be a great component for warding off mal de ojo, or the evil eye.

Agua de Florida can be found in botánicas, spiritual shops, metaphysical stores, and apothecaries or herbal shops. You can even make your own Florida Water at home using flowers, herbs, citrus, essential oils, sacred resins, and rubbing alcohol. Ask an adult to help you with this recipe.

Include equal parts rubbing alcohol and water. The alcohol is used to infuse all the ingredients together and extract their amazing qualities and benefits. You can use whatever herbs and other ingredients you have on hand or the ones you intuitively feel the need to include. Great options are rose petals, which have the highest frequency of love, cinnamon to attract abundance and represent the fire element, citrus fruits like orange, lime, and lemon, and lavender for love and healing.

Once you've got everything together in a jar with a lid, shake it up and place it on your altar or a sacred place in your home where it will steep for at least one moon cycle (approximately 29.5 days) or more. When it's ready, shake it up again and strain into a small bottle. I recommend a spritz bottle for easy sprays. Only a little should be used at a time—it goes a long way.

There are so many uses for Florida Water. Everything from using it as a hand sanitizer to a protection for your aura before you leave the house for the day and cleansing it when you return home, or as a great cleanser for your home, spritzing it or adding a splash to mop water to energetically clean floors, windows, doors, etc. It's also great to use right before meditation, yoga, journaling, or chanting to help elevate the practice.

Florida Water is a wonderful ingredient for baños and limpias, as previously mentioned, but it's just as powerful when used in barridas, a spiritual practice that consists of a curanderx praying over someone as they sweep the person from head to feet with various herbs and other sacred materials. Typically, the Florida Water is sprayed over the person's body by an experienced curanderx gently three times at the top, middle, and bottom of the body. Use the spritzer, and of course, be sure you have the other person's consent.

WHERE TO FIND ESSENTIAL ELEMENTS

Botánicas are religious shops often found in areas where large Latine populations live. These shops carry all the essential elements needed for spiritual work, including statues of deities, candles, a variety of herbs, oils, and even soaps. Apothecaries are shops offering herbal remedies and are also great places to visit to get all your ingredients. You may also be able to find what you need at special events during celebrations like Indigenous Peoples' Day, which occurs in October. Look for local festivals in your area. Vendors selling various spiritual tools, clothing items, and objects of symbolism gather to share in the celebration.

If you don't have a local botánica or apothecary and don't want to wait to attend an event, start by looking around your home. You'll be amazed to find that a lot of ingredients and tools used in spiritual practices can be found in your kitchen cabinet or bathroom. Things like cinnamon, basil, bay leaves, citrus fruits, and salts can typically be found at home or at your local grocery store. You do not have to buy these items from a metaphysical store for them to work. They are just as magical if you buy them from a grocery store or farmer's market. Remember, the power within these items is ignited with your intention and purpose for using them. So let's get ready to create some magic!

Herbs

. . . . ✳ . . . .

The beauty of Mother Earth or Pachamama, as the Indigenous peoples of the Andes call her, is that she gifts us with a wide variety of herbs that can be used for nearly every ailment. Remember that these spiritual practices are a complement to your regular doctor's visits.

In Indigenous Latine spiritual practices, herbs are used in limpias, baños, and barridas. Depending on the intention of the practice, different herbs are used to release anger, stress, and other ailments. The herbs can also be used to enhance spiritual connections to ancestors and other guides in the spirit world, and to attract or invite in things you'd like to manifest, such as love and money.

Herbs can be mixed with water and other ingredients for limpias and baños or to anoint candles. You can even place a small bowl of herbs on your altar as an offering to ancestors or to communicate a need to the Universe or show gratitude.

Some examples include holy basil, which has been used for centuries for love, wealth, and uplifting energy. Alfalfa is a great herb to use if you're doing work around abundance, money, prosperity, and even to fight against hunger. This herb can be used to create money altars with the intention of protection from hunger and poverty by sprinkling some on a dish with coins and dollars. Anise is used to ward off the evil eye and can be quite powerful when paired with rue either in the herbal or water form. Camphor is great for dream interpretation and elevating psychic awareness. It's also a great herb to work with when moving into a new space, whether for home or work. Dandelion leaf can help when communicating with spirits and seeking healing, protection, and purification. This herb can be placed in a small pouch and carried with you to manifest what you want to invite into your life.

The list of magical herbs is endless. There are thousands, maybe even millions, of herbs available to us for spiritual maintenance. Start with what you have in your spice cabinet, or look at the teas you have in your kitchen. There's a good chance it is full of magical herbs and spices.

Flowers

Have you ever been outside and felt the energy of the flowers surrounding you? Flowers are believed to have the highest form of energy and have been used in spiritual practices since the beginning of time. Their energy is so palpable that placing a bouquet of flowers in a room can immediately elevate the space. Receiving flowers from a loved one impacts us on a cellular level, pumping up endorphins and serotonin. Our floral friends have been found to boost creativity and improve mood and overall health by easing stress, anxiety, and even depression. Flowers also bring pleasure and feelings of gratitude. Having fresh flowers in your bedroom is a great way to continuously renew the energy in your space. Trust! You'll feel it.

Just like herbs, there is a wide variety of flowers used in spiritual practices for different intentions. Roses, specifically red roses, contain the highest frequency of any plant, which is 320 megahertz (MHz), according to the standard unit of frequency in the International System of Units. So aside from how beautiful they are and their skincare and health benefits, roses can produce amazing results when added to limpias, baños, and other spiritual practices. You can also use rose water for quick spurts of elevating energy and the frequency of love in your life if you don't have fresh or dried flowers.

Plants

A supreme zemí, or god, in Taíno Indigenous wisdom is Yukahú, the lord of life, who is associated with the sun and the sky. He is the light and life energy, and Taínos believe the plants absorb that energy through the process of photosynthesis, in which plants absorb water and carbon dioxide to give off oxygen and form carbohydrates or sugars. The plant most directly associated with Yukahú is yuca, a root vegetable often used to make casabe bread. When Yukahú's sacred energy is absorbed by the plants, it creates a passageway for humans to use it too. This is why plants, herbs, and flowers are such key ingredients in spiritual rituals.

Shamans believe that certain plants, like rosemary and rue, help to keep evil spirits from nearing the home. These plants are also used in spiritual baths and barridas.

Lemongrass, bay leaf, and castor are other plants commonly used in Indigenous spiritual practices. Aloe is another plant with strong spiritual ties. When aloe powder is used during a spiritual ritual, it is believed to send protection to loved ones. Ancient Taíno plants like anamu were used in cleansing baths and believed to relieve ailments like rheumatism and arthritis, as well as ease symptoms of depression.

Oils

Ancient Egyptians are credited with being the first to begin using essential oils for traditional medicines and perfumes. These oils derived from plant extracts have been used in other parts of the world, too, in spiritual ceremonies and for medicinal use. In Central America and the Caribbean, amyris essential oil has been used in spiritual practices and as traditional medicine for centuries along with sweetwood, which is also native to Mexico.

Palo santo is a powerful, high-frequency oil and can be used to stimulate the senses before spiritual practices by smelling it and dabbing a little on your wrist. Frankincense essential oil is also great for enhancing meditation and strengthening the spiritual connection.

Many Indigenous spiritual practices include the use of a mixture of various oils to make unique blends. Ginger, star anise, cedarwood, and clove are popular blends to help ground and center. Rose, lavender, and basil essential oils can be combined to raise vibrations and inspire feelings of love, tranquility, and abundance. In curanderismo practices, the essential oils are placed in a cobalt blue glass bottle that holds and amplifies the energy and may be paired with other ingredients like crystals and minerals. Do not ingest any oils.

Shells, Gemstones, and Feathers

∴❋∴

Throughout Mexico, the conch shell has been used for spiritual practices as an instrument, shell trumpet, or wind jewel. The shell's deep horn can be played using the natural shell or a ceramic shell. In many depictions of Quetzalcoatl, the Aztec deity known as the god of the wind, he wore a conch shell. An ancient myth credits Quetzalcoatl with spreading the joy of music throughout the land by gathering the musicians and singers that lived in the house of Father Sun and spreading them all over the Earth. The conch shell emblem he wore symbolizes the deity's direct connection to music.

The abalone shell is considered a sacred symbol of the sea that can calm emotions, release negativity, and offer guidance. While most abalone are found in cold coastal waters, white abalone are found in the Pacific Ocean from California to Mexico.

Yemaya, a prominent and beloved spirit of various African diasporic traditions and beliefs, is the queen of the sea, and she is often shown wearing cowrie shells, which can be found all over the world. The shells were used for currency and held spiritual significance.

Shells can represent the earth, water, and air elements and can be used as a spiritual tool to catch the ash that falls as sacred herbs are burned for purification. As noted before, they can also be used as instruments. Many practices include blowing into the shell to hear the deep horn sounds floating into the air as you face, honor, and acknowledge the four corners—north, east, south, and west. This was often the beginning of spiritual ceremonies.

Gemstones are also associated with many spiritual practices as they are of the earth and are believed to have souls that can help support and guide humans along their journey. In the Dominican Republic, the rare blue larimar stone is used in spiritual practices to symbolize peace and healing and is known as the Love Stone. Curanderismo practices may include placing rose quartz arrowheads pointing outward to symbolize the spread of love, compassion, and blessings.

Feathers are also important, as they are worn in ceremonies as headpieces and with other spiritual garb. The feathers are a powerful symbol of honor and our connection to the earth, to Spirit, and to birds. They represent wisdom and freedom, and if you see feathers often, it is believed that an angel or a divine ancestor is communicating with you.

CHAPTER FIVE
ANCESTORS AND ALTARS

Connecting to Your Ancestors

⋯⋯⋯⋯⋯❋⋯⋯⋯⋯⋯

Ancestors are people who lived a human life and are a part of our family but have transitioned to the spirit world. While they have journeyed out of human form, their energy, or soul, is still very much alive and vibrant and can help support our journeys. Connecting to them can be as simple as speaking their name and saying you need their support or guidance. It's good to remember that not all of our ancestors will support us, so adding words like "benevolent," "compassionate," or "kind-hearted" before saying "ancestor" helps to focus your intention on communicating with those who truly have your best interest in mind. For example:

I call on my benevolent ancestors to come forth and assist me as I navigate this challenge I now face.

Remember that your words are quite powerful, so use them carefully to get the best outcome when tapping into your magic.

It's important to connect with our ancestors because they have experienced human life already, and their wisdom could help to guide us during our lifetime. Someday, you will be an ancestor, and someone in your family lineage may call on you to support them. For most of our ancestors, it's an honor to be called upon by a family member who is still experiencing human life. It is why Día de los Muertos, or the Day of the Dead, is celebrated annually throughout Mexico on November 1 and 2. Building altars and placing photos and other items symbolic of our ancestors shows that we honor and respect their wisdom and guidance.

Ancestors may also try to communicate with us in our dreams or through repetitive numbers, or angel numbers, which are number sequences that usually contain three or four repetitive numbers. You may suddenly smell your grandmother's perfume, or a song she loved begins playing when you think of her. These are examples of the ways our ancestors will speak to us. Trust that their communication is very real, and your ability to listen and hear their messages will expand. Connecting with the elements around us in our daily lives is another way to open a clear pathway of conversation with our ancestors.

Healing Yourself Means Healing Your Ancestral Lineage

We carry the spirit of our ancestors with us throughout our lives. If your lineage has suffered greatly through various trials and tribulations, you may feel it in your life too. Rest assured that doing this work or even desiring to learn how to tap into your spirituality is

already healing your ancestral lineage. It takes one person to break the cycle of suffering in a family. It may not be the easiest task depending on the depth of obstacles your ancestral lineage may have faced, but it is absolutely possible.

For generations, it has been believed that when one person in the family heals, other members of the family heal too. This person is sometimes referred to as a cycle-breaker in the family. As they heal, they acknowledge that their ancestors did the best they could, but it's time to live in a new way. It is believed that when we do this, we heal seven generations before us and seven generations after us. The cycle-breaker shifts the history and future of the family. If this sounds overwhelming, it's okay. It is a lot to think about. But it's also beautiful to know that you were gifted this human life, and through your journey, you have chosen to heal. As you do, your family heals too. But remember: it starts with you.

Begin by connecting to your benevolent ancestors whether you've met them in life or not. You can honor them by placing their photo or something that belonged to them on your altar. You can also acknowledge them by name, letting them know that you feel their presence in your life. Once you're connected, you can ask permission to heal the lineage simply by doing spiritual work to heal yourself, and you may ask for assistance in doing so. Your healing is their healing. Focus on healing yourself, and the rest will fall into divine place.

Creating an Altar

⁕

One way to call on your ancestors and the four corners while practicing to strengthen that intuitive muscle is by creating altars. I have altars all over my home. Some represent very personal things, like self-love or money, while others may be a physical representation of the ancestors I believe are with me the most. Creating altar space is a show of gratitude for their presence in my life. It is also a recognition of the understanding that life goes way beyond the physical, and that we can work with and gain support from energy that doesn't have a physical manifestation.

Regardless of the purpose of your altar, it should include representation of the four elements, which are also symbolic of the four corners or cardinal directions. Adding a candle can symbolize the fire (south) element, as well as air (north). Plants or flowers are great for the earth (east) element, and a bowl or small glass of water (west) brings in that element. The water in a vase of flowers can also symbolize that element. For more on essential elements, see chapter four.

Altars can be both big and small, and they can even travel with you. You can create at-home altars for ancestors, self-love, and so much more, but make sure to keep them tidy. This communicates to the Universe and/ or your ancestors that you are aware of a Higher Power guiding you through life, and a way to show gratitude for that guidance is by keeping your altars clean. Give them a quick refresh with light dusting or by changing the glass of water weekly, monthly, or seasonally. Listen to your intuition telling you it's time. Or tap into that connection to all things, and you may even hear a whisper from the flowers sitting on your altar that they need fresh water, or it may be your ancestors asking for an offering—maybe something they enjoyed when they were alive like rice, fruit, or even coffee beans.

When traveling, you can keep a small altar with you by simply having four things to represent the elements and cardinal directions and something to symbolize your intention. If you are creating a protection altar so you feel safe as you travel, consider having a small bottle of Florida Water, a crystal-like onyx or black tourmaline to represent protection (and the earth element), a feather to symbolize air, and a lighter and an unlit candle to represent fire. When you arrive at your destination, find a spot that calls to you (use your intuition) and place your altar there for the duration of your stay. As you set up your altar, pray, sing, and speak your intentions out loud. What you say is a very personal journey. This is your conversation with the Universe that cannot be dictated by anyone else. It comes from your soul. If you're unsure of where to start, simply give thanks as you place each item on your altar. Thank the spiritual tools you've chosen for your altar for their sacred presence, and thank the Universe, God, the Higher Power, for the guidance and protection you receive in your life. Imagine a beautiful glowing light shining brightly from the altar that you can carry with you throughout your travels.

If you are gathering with your bruja friends or with a group of spiritualists like you, a beautiful altar can be created by the collective group. Everyone can bring offerings to add to the altar, which will be positioned in the center of the room where you gather. In our digital world, you can also do this virtually with one or more of the participants holding space by creating the altar wherever they are, representing the whole group.

The materials needed for your altar start with the four elements. Once you have something to represent each one, you can add other items to customize your altar and its purpose. Additional items may include photos of ancestors or loved ones who have transitioned beyond this physical human life, or things they loved like perfume, a specific food or drink, or even a piece of jewelry. Herbs or crystals that coincide with your intention can also be added to your altar. For example, if you're creating a money altar, consider adding a small bowl of tulsi, or holy basil, which coincides with abundance and has been used for thousands of years as a symbol of wealth in many cultures.

If you're seeking guidance using an altar, you can add something specific to the question you're asking. For example, if you're undecided about which after-school club to join and really don't know which to choose, think about creating an altar and adding representation of the four elements alongside things that symbolize the various academic clubs you're considering. These could be pictures or logos representing the various clubs. As you place the items on your altar, speak your intentions out loud, sparking magic in the air as you do so. You could say something like, "Great Spirit, I seek guidance about which academic club to sign up for. They all sound interesting, but I want to choose the one that will benefit me most." Then light your candle or burn some incense to represent the fire element and spark your intention. Remember to always use caution when working with fire and get an adult's help. Sitting in meditation in front of your altar for even a moment may deliver the answers to your questions.

Don't worry if the answers don't come right away. Sometimes it takes a little longer to gain clarity and the answers may not be easily found, but if you are open to receiving the guidance, you will. Just be on the lookout for it because the Universe often communicates with us in a wide variety of ways.

How to Maintain Your Altar

· · · · · · · · · · ❊ · · · · · · · · · ·

Maintaining and refreshing your altar is a way to keep the magic strong and your intentions clear. Remember that you can tap into your intuition to discover when your altar, or altars, needs a quick refresh. You can even time it with the changing of the seasons and not only refresh your altar physically by removing everything on it and cleaning the surface, but also cleanse it spiritually with Florida Water, which you can use to wipe down the surface and all the items. As you spray the Florida Water, take each item and allow it to be encompassed, thanking the water for its cleansing powers. There are so many household items typically found around our home that can be used in spiritual practices if you don't have Florida Water. Start by looking at the spice rack in your kitchen. Herbs like basil have been used in spiritual practices to invite love. Cinnamon symbolizes abundance when used in spiritual rituals. Or you can fill a glass with regular tap water and pray over it, saying something like:

Thank you, Spirit, for my life.
Bless this water so it may soak up any negative energy,
creating space for peace, happiness, joy, and protection.

When you place your items back on the altar, do so intuitively. Don't give it much thought. Just lift each item and watch where your hand naturally places it. Do this enough, and you may begin hearing or feeling signals from the items on your altar as to where they want to be placed. You'll be amazed at the beauty of your intuitively arranged altars.

CHAPTER SIX

THE MOON AND SUN

Working with the Moon

The moon contains a massive amount of energy that directly affects us. The Taínos, the Indigenous people of the Caribbean, praised the Diosa Luna, or the moon goddess. Folklore indicated that the sun, moon, and stars all rose from caves, and while the sun was at its peak, the Diosa Luna hid in the cave until it was time for her to rise in the night sky. She symbolizes a joyful tranquility and wears a big smile. Atabey, the queen mother of the zemís, or gods, was also symbolic of the moon since she is the goddess of motherhood, birther of all things. She represents fertility, birth, creation, and the menstrual cycle, which coincides with the twenty-eight-day cycle of the moon.

The Taínos lived life by the phases of the moon, which helped guide them in community work like agriculture and in celebrations like marriage and childbirth. Stories of women becoming pregnant after praising the moon goddess were common among the Taínos.

This was also true for the Mayans, who represented parts of Mexico, Honduras, and El Salvador, as well as Guatemala and Belize. Ixchel represented their moon goddess and was associated with fertility and procreation. The Inca, or Indigenous people of South America, praised Mama Quilla, the Incan moon goddess, who was considered a defender of women. The way they worked with the moon was often tied directly to its cycles.

Full Moon

·············❋·············

Full moons have been linked to impulsive behavior in people because at its peak the moon's energy intensifies, and seemingly so does ours. Some may feel extremely emotional or have heightened awareness during full moons. It's like that big, beautiful, bright ball in the night sky creates a direct connection to Spirit, and our ability to receive messages and guidance amplifies.

In shamanic practices, it's believed that the full moon energy pulls our deepest thoughts and emotions to the surface, allowing us to come face-to-face with what we need to heal and release. It parallels how the full moon's gravitational pull impacts our waters, the element shamans associate with our innermost thoughts and emotions.

This idea is widely practiced today with the full moon being associated with letting go or shedding old skin, which is a metaphor for releasing all the things that no longer serve you. This could be a pattern that you've noticed occurring in your life. If it's something you can control and dismiss, then let it go under the light of a full moon.

FULL MOON RITUALS

Indigenous full moon rituals include honoring the four elements, so that is a great place to start when thinking about your own full moon rituals. Representations of the earth, air, fire, and water were used to pay homage to our lunar companion and still play a major role in full moon rituals today.

While Indigenous ancestors typically gathered as a community for full moon rituals, there are ways to work with the moon individually or in smaller groups within your own family and friends. Limpias are a great way to create full moon rituals at home using the four elements and are centered around cleansing negative and stagnant energy from you and your space. Limpias mean "cleansings" in Spanish, serving to release what's no longer useful to you and renewing and refreshing your energy. You can find moon limpias in chapter ten.

Each full moon, like each new moon, is associated with a zodiac sign. You can use this to help you set focused intentions with the moon. For example, the full moon in Taurus is a good time to shed any limiting beliefs around money so you can begin embracing your abundance, regardless of the circumstances you were born into. Full moon rituals intended to shift your mind, body, and spirit from a place of lack into a vibration of abundance can be transformative for your life and healing for your ancestral lineage. Doing this during a Taurus full moon is especially powerful because the second sign of the zodiac is known as the sign of abundance, and when grounding into this earth sign, it is believed that you can manifest just about anything. The full moon gives you the power to cleanse your energy before inviting in those transformative, abundant Taurus vibes.

Regardless of what zodiac sign the full moon is in, you can honor yourself with a beautiful limpia to renew and recharge your energy. If you want to pair it with a zodiac sign, simply research the components that align nicely with that sign, like the candle color, flower, or crystals that are associated with it.

New Moon

· · · · · · · · ❋ · · · · · · · ·

Unlike the full moon, which is great for letting go, the new moon is all about inviting in the things you want to manifest in your life. Indigenous traditions often included planting seeds on the new moon and gathering to share wisdom through storytelling. The new moon is the beautiful open space created by letting go and releasing under the full moon. It is the ripe soil from which beautiful things can grow.

The new moon is a dark moon, so you won't be able to see it in the night sky like the full moon. But just because we can't see something doesn't mean it isn't there or doesn't exist. So keep that in mind when working with the powerful, mysterious new moon.

NEW MOON RITUALS

New Moons are invisible moons. Unlike its evident and boisterous full moon phase, the new moon isn't visible in the night sky. It's a beautiful way to symbolize all the magic that occurs out of plain sight. It's also a great time to set intentions on what you want to invite into your life. What are you trying to manifest? What do you want to take from the dream world into your reality?

Like full moons, new moons are also associated with various zodiac signs, and that can influence your ritual. But overall, new moons are a great time to create a spiritual baño to complement your wishes. Baños differ from limpias because you soak in them instead of pouring them over your body. You can find a new moon baño ritual in chapter ten.

If you want to watch your dreams manifest over time, keep a new moon manifestation journal. During each new moon, write ten wishes, read them out loud, and say thank you to the Universe for bringing these things into your life. Then put your journal away. Don't fixate on the things you've written in it. The idea is that whatever you wish for on the new moon will begin manifesting over the next six months before the full moon in that same zodiac sign. For example, if you set intentions and wishes on the new moon in Scorpio, watch what happens until the full moon in Scorpio. You may see some of those wishes come true, or you may notice new pathways opening to make them a reality.

Lunar Eclipses

Lunar eclipses occur when the shadow of the Earth is cast onto the moon from the sun, and it is considered a time of spiritual transformation. As we previously discussed, the moon impacts things on planet Earth, including us. Some report that life becomes chaotic during eclipses, and ancestral spiritual traditions urge you to lean in and invite the transformation that's occurring. Elders from the Laguna-Acoma Pueblo tribe of New Mexico advised their kin not to fear a lunar eclipse, but instead to embrace it. If fear was felt, it would indicate wrongdoing. They pray to cornmeal, meditate, and flow with the transformation. In some Indigenous traditions, sacred naming ceremonies would take place during a lunar eclipse.

LUNAR ECLIPSE RITUALS

Lunar eclipses pack a powerfully energetic punch, making it a great time to do spiritual work. Here's a lunar eclipse ritual that's easy to do, doesn't require a lot of materials, and can be quite impactful on your journey.

1. Sit in meditation by an open window or outside, if you can. If not, a comfortable spot you enjoy will do just fine. You can sit on a meditation pillow, a yoga mat, or in a chair with your feet flat on the ground.

2. Light a candle. Any color will work depending on your intention. For this ritual, let's focus on self-love. A pink candle would work nicely! Remember to use caution when working with open flames, and ask for an adult's assistance.

3. As you light the candle, focus on your intention. For this ritual, you are reminding yourself of how divine you are and how your existence in this life is a blessing not only to you but to others as well.

4. Close your eyes and chant, "I am divine." Repeat it seven times before inhaling deeply and exhaling with a sigh out of your mouth.

5. Sit in meditation and allow those words to flow through you from the top of your head to your toes.

6. Silently continue repeating "I am divine" as you imagine scanning your body from head to toe.

7. You are divine! Embody it.

Supermoons and Blue Moons

⋯⋯⋯⋯⋯ ✳ ⋯⋯⋯⋯⋯

Supermoons occur when the moon's orbit is closest to Earth during a full moon. Spiritually, supermoons are believed to have amplified energy that helps us connect with nature and our highest selves. Indigenous spiritual traditions often included rituals and ceremonies during this time because of the potent energy.

Blue moons differ from supermoons because they occur every two or three years when there is an extra full moon in a year. There is the rare instance when there is a blue moon supermoon, which occurs about every ten years and spiritually speaking is believed to be a powerful time to do shadow work, facing your hidden fears and deepest traumas, and healing.

Working with the Sun

⋯⋯⋯⋯ ✳ ⋯⋯⋯⋯

The sun has been worshipped as a deity or god by many Indigenous groups. The Taíno symbol for the sun, el Sol de Jayuya or Sol Taíno, is one of the most popular symbols of the Indigenous Caribbean people. This powerful symbol represented the Taínos' spiritual beliefs and connection to nature. They honored the cosmic energy of Yukahú, the lord of life, who is associated with the sun and the sky. The Incas from Peru believed they were direct descendants of the sun, Lord Sun or Apu Inti. The Sun Dance is considered one of the most important religious ceremonies practiced by the Plains Indians of North America.

The sun has been praised as one of the highest deities due to its enriching, nourishing abilities in helping things grow. Its life-giving abundance was known to heal and create peace. It is the reflection of our own soul.

One of the strongest ways to work with the sun spiritually is to wake up before it rises and begin a ritual-like prayer, meditation, or gentle movement to greet the new day. This helps to connect the light in you with the light of the day. As we charge our souls with solar energy, we reflect that light within others.

If you can go outside and face east before the sun rises, gently close your eyes and focus on your breathing. Meditate, chant, sing, or pray. Go deeply within to connect to the energy of those early morning hours, considered the ambrosial hours between 4:00 a.m. and 6:00 a.m. when the veil between us and God is believed to be at its thinnest. With such a close connection, we give an offering by practicing spirituality as the sun is rising. Once it has risen, get up and raise your arms high to the sky. Inhale deeply before exhaling slowly and folding forward at the hip, bringing your hands to meet the ground, if you can. If not, you can touch your knees, shins, or ankles. Bend your knees slightly to push your body back upright and repeat. This movement is not only awakening your physical body, it is also a physical offering and salutation to the sun.

The power of the sun can be used to balance your third eye chakra as well. The third eye chakra is located between your eyebrows and symbolizes our ability to see the bigger picture of our lives, envisioning what our ideal lives would look like and taking inspired action to bring that vision into our reality. When you sit with the sun rays warming this energy center, or chakra, it can have a beautifully grounding and centering effect.

Sit with your eyes closed and your face pointing in the direction of the sun. Feel the connection of the sun's warmth on your third eye and sit there for about seven minutes if you can. As you sit, you may receive visions or inspiring ideas. Just take note of them and allow them to come and go like the rays of the sun on a cloudy day. When you open your eyes, thank the sun for its power, love, and warmth. Do this as often as possible. The sun's rays offer natural vitamin D for our bodies. So step outside, find a sunny spot, and absorb the sun's beautifully charged-up energy.

SOLAR ECLIPSE RITUALS

A solar eclipse occurs when the moon is between the Earth and the sun and creates a shadow. This astrological event carries powerfully transformative energy, just like lunar eclipses. Many Indigenous cultures believed that a solar eclipse was an optimal time to perform cleansing rituals to inspire introspection, symbolize renewal, and gain protective energy. It is not advised to begin new projects during a solar eclipse or make impulsive decisions. And make sure to watch your words and temper. Eclipses can turn our emotions inside out, and before you know it, you're lashing out at someone when your message could have been delivered in a better way. So be mindful of your emotions during a solar eclipse. If you're feeling particularly hot-tempered, take some time in solitude to reflect on your emotions. Watch as they flow like waves with some crashing down and some rising and falling with ease. Becoming the watcher of your emotions is essential to being able to manage them.

SEASONAL RITUALS
(WINTER, SPRING, SUMMER, FALL)

Seasonal spiritual rituals can be done by intentionally shifting your space with each new season. For example, my maternal grandmother had a seasonal ritual of changing drapes and bedding in every bedroom in her home at the start of each new season. You could feel the energy shift this created and how it left the rooms not only physically clean but also energetically refreshed.

CHAPTER SEVEN
RITUALS

Modern-day brujas are adapting the practices of our ancestors and honoring their traditions while also making them uniquely our own. The intuition is strong, and when you learn to hear your intuitive voice, it's time to listen. This voice can be the driving force of our spiritual practices and the ingredients, tools, and methods we use. Understanding the significance of various rituals is also important so that you know which ones to use at various times and situations.

Spiritual Cleansing

Cleansing rituals or rites should be incorporated into everyday life for spiritual upkeep and maintenance. Remember that these rituals do not have to be taxing emotionally. Incorporating cleansing rituals in your practice is a way to keep you healthy mentally, physically, and spiritually.

An easy one is to spray a little Florida Water on your hands and then place them in front of your face as you inhale before raising and brushing them over your head. You can repeat this three times before leaving the house in the morning. It clears your mind of negative thoughts and can act as a barrier throughout your day against lower vibrational emotions from others, including anger and envy. You can also burn candles and set the intention that the flame will symbolize the purification of your space from negative and stagnant energy. Whenever working with open flames, safety is first. Ask an adult to assist you.

An even easier practical magic cleansing ritual you can use is to carry a gemstone with you throughout your day that is used for purification, such as clear quartz or selenite. Many places sell gemstone jewelry like earrings, necklaces, and bracelets, which are a great way to stay on top of your spiritual maintenance and be fashionable all at once. And don't forget that a good spiritual baño or limpia could be just what you need to cleanse your spirit and feel renewed.

Spiritual Protection

❖

Similar to spiritual cleansing, protecting yourself spiritually is extremely important to ward off evil eye, or mal de ojo, and negativity. You can wear evil eye jewelry to protect yourself or keep it in your home for protection there. Holding a gemstone that signifies spiritual protection can also be useful. Consider carrying a black tourmaline stone in your pocket, purse, or bag. You can place a protective shield around yourself by passing a selenite stick around your body from head to toe. Florida Water is also powerful here, as it can be used to cleanse the body spiritually and to protect it. The use of palo santo can increase the protection of your space and yourself or objects. Sage is believed to cleanse the space while palo santo locks in all the goodness of that cleanse to prolong protection and good energy. You don't even have to light it! You can find sage and palo santo in liquid form and spray them, or they can be used in oil form. Also, reminding yourself that you are protected is a big one. If you are feeling vulnerable or exposed to situations where you don't feel protected, you can speak out loud to Spirit, your ancestors, and your spirit team, saying something like, "I am protected, guided, and safe." Repeat it until you feel it and believe it. Your spirit team is listening.

MAL DE OJO

Mal de ojo translates in English to mean evil eye, and it is believed to be a serious spiritual ailment in places like Mexico, the Caribbean, Latin America, West Africa, and parts of the Middle East. Others believe it's a superstition. Many cultures believe mal de ojo can lead to illness and misfortune for the recipient. Since mal de ojo is often sent from one person to another unintentionally, it's important that we protect ourselves through spiritual maintenance and the use of spiritual symbolism like the eye symbol seen around the world. It is worn to ward off negative energy from those who are hating on you and your successes, and even people who truly admire you but don't realize that their self-comparisons breed envy and may send evil eye to you. The belief is that when a person looks at another in the eye with envy, jealousy, malicious intent, or even admiration, the recipient receives evil eye, or mal de ojo. Some cultures also believe mal de ojo can be transferred from one person to another via tone of voice.

In the Yucatán Peninsula, the Indigenous Mayan communities believed that the young were especially vulnerable to mal de ojo because they weren't yet resilient enough to repel it. But adults could also find themselves at the receiving end of the evil eye.

Wearing mal de ojo jewelry or using home decor can add a layer of spiritual protection to the person using it and the space it's in. This symbol helps protect from mal de ojo and symptoms like fever, nausea, vomiting, fatigue, insomnia, loss of appetite, and bad luck. In children, additional symptoms may include diarrhea and excessive crying.

Various Indigenous groups even had their own rituals to rid or protect someone from mal de ojo. The native people of the Yucatán would tie a red string bracelet around the right wrist of a young person to repel the evil eye. The color was strategically chosen as a hue symbolizing potent and alluring energy. When someone wears it, the evil eye is absorbed within the bracelet. Some communities insist their children wear the bracelet until they are old enough to speak up for themselves.

Traditional Mayan spiritual doctors, or curanderxs, diagnose mal de ojo by passing a raw egg all around the body of a sick child and then cracking it. If evil eye is detected, the curanderx will facilitate a spiritual limpia using different plants and other ingredients.

Manifestation

M anifestation is all the buzz, with many people wondering how to attract the things into their lives that they most desire. One important thing to know about manifestation is that you won't get everything you want simply because you want it. Our wishes and intentions must align with our true essence, our soul purpose, and if they don't, then no matter how much you want it, the Universe won't allow manifestation to enter your life. Or it may enter your life to teach you a lesson you wouldn't learn otherwise. This is different from failure. You can try your hand at something and fail, and it doesn't mean it isn't aligned with you; it may just mean you have to try again. So make sure you're clear on what you want to manifest and why. Whatever you manifest should be something that elevates your human experience in a way that doesn't harm anyone else or yourself. Instead, what you manifest could impact the collective if it comes to fruition in your life. For example, you may want to manifest a new bike, which would make it easier to get around town when visiting friends while lessening the need for your parents to drive you everywhere. Your manifestation has had a positive impact on more than just you.

Manifestation rituals can take place in many forms. You can create a baño to manifest things on the new moon, or you can create a manifestation altar that includes items symbolizing what you desire to bring into your reality. A great and well-known manifestation technique is a vision board. By seeing images of the things you want to manifest repeatedly over time, you will bring those things into your life. It could be a few months or years. The most important thing is to believe that when you set an intention of manifesting something in your life, it will come to be if it is aligned with your spirit. That's where listening to your intuition and connecting to Spirit, your benevolent ancestors, and your spirit team is important to help guide you in the right direction.

Affirmations are a great way to amplify your manifestations. So if you see the bike you want to manifest on the street as someone else is riding by, you can look at it and acknowledge that it's already yours. It's just a matter of time before a bike enters your life. Believe it. Feel it. Trust it.

CHAPTER EIGHT
MEDITATION

Meditation is a beautiful way to go inward and deeply connect with yourself. There are various ways to meditate, so if one doesn't suit you, try a different approach. Sitting in stillness and connecting to the breath is a beautiful way to ground yourself if you're feeling anxious, stressed, or overwhelmed with emotions. It's easy for our minds to wander, thinking a million thoughts. So if we find our way back to our breath each time we notice our restless mind trying to take over the meditation, it will help us to stay present and just be.

Connecting to the Breath

Try sitting on a yoga mat or a pillow on the floor with your back straight and your chin slightly pointing down toward your chest. This elongates the spine, allowing energy to flow freely through the center of your body and each chakra. We'll get to that in just a bit. Place your hands gently on your legs with the palms facing up. This indicates you want to receive spiritual guidance and messages from the Universe. Close your eyes and just breathe. You don't have to breathe in any particular way. Just allow your breath to come and go as it may without trying to change it. Observe this flow entering and exiting your body. This is a life force, and it is a miraculous thing to be able to breathe. Acknowledge the miracle and feel gratitude for being able to take those breaths. Sit and observe your breath for as long as you can. Once you notice other thoughts coming in, return to the breath once more before opening your eyes. It may have only been thirty seconds, and that's okay. The next time you try this practice you may be able to sit for one whole minute or maybe three until the time is no longer an issue at all.

Soul-Journeying
Meditation

...............❋...............

When you're able to meditate for longer periods of time by observing the flow of the breath, you can now try going a bit deeper. In Indigenous spiritual wisdom, journeying through meditation was believed to be possible. It's when your soul travels to other places and times through the mind. This soul journeying can be assisted by cleansing your space and yourself before beginning your meditation ritual. You can use sage or palo santo or simply spray a bit of Florida Water on your hands, inhaling the calming scent a few times and gently rubbing your hands down your body from head to toe, setting your intention to journey during your meditation as you do so. You can also play music to help guide you along your soul journey. Remember that music is often associated with the wind in Indigenous traditions, so the sound of the melody and instrumentation can carry your soul to the far reaches of your mind where self-discovery and healing exist. Chanting can also help amplify the power behind soul-journeying meditations, and essential oils can help awaken the spirit to receiving the messages and lessons discovered through this practice.

A simple drumbeat or the soft sound of a flute can carry you deep into a journeying meditation. As you sit with your eyes closed, begin focusing on the sound of the music and allow its waves to carry you away. Trust that you are safe and that you are on a mission of self-discovery and awareness. The Universe and your spirit team will help guide you. If you're unsure of this, say it out loud: "As I go inward for this soul journey, I ask the Universe and my spirit team to guide and protect me." Verbalizing those words releases your magic into the air like stardust. You have connected with the Universe by stating this intention and asking to be guided. Now, as you sit with your eyes closed and your heart connected to the beat of the drum or the flute's song, you become the observer of your soul's journey. It may not all make sense at first. Little flashes of images may come up. Some familiar, some brand new. Or you may suddenly see the face of someone you know—a loved one or a friend, or even maybe a frenemy. Don't try to figure it out; just take notice and allow the journey to flow. You may become so connected to your soul journey that your physical body reacts, like you suddenly feel a smile form on your face because your soul has journeyed to a place that makes you happy. You could also feel a tear rolling down your cheek if you've seen an image of something that makes you sad or disappointed. It's okay if those things come up too. When we can face the things that make us feel sad, disappointed, angry, and so on, therein lies the lesson. We can learn something from them, and once we do, we transform the experience from something bad or hurtful into something that has strengthened us moving forward. Our life experiences help us to gain wisdom, but they do not have to define who we are. Soul-journeying meditation is a wonderful way to truly connect with yourself and the Great Mystery that is helping to cocreate your life.

Grounding Meditation

❊

If you're feeling out of sorts or off-balance, try this grounding meditation to help you calm down and reconnect. You can sit in the meditation pose we've been discussing, or feel free to sit in a chair, on a bench, or even on your bed as long as your feet can fully connect with the floor or the ground beneath them. Place your hands on your legs with the palms down for grounding. Close your eyes and take three cleansing breaths by inhaling deeply through your nose and exhaling with a gentle sigh out of your mouth. With each exhale, feel your body letting go and relaxing deeply. After the third round of cleansing breaths, return to your normal breathing with your eyes closed. Imagine a beautiful, glowing light forming at the top of your head, your crown. See it shining like a spotlight—you're the star of this show! As the light brightens, imagine it expanding and slowly illuminating your body from the top of your crown and down through all parts of your body all the way to your toes. Then imagine roots growing from beneath your feet and toes and watch as those roots travel all the way to the center of the Earth. Breathe that in. Focus on the visualization for a moment before watching those roots travel back up from the center of the Earth to your feet, and begin making the slightest movements by wiggling your toes and your fingers to bring yourself back into the room before slowly opening your eyes. Put your hands one on top of the other over your heart chakra at the center of your chest, take a deep breath in through your nose, and allow the exhale to leave through your mouth. If you feel compelled to move, get up and shake your arms and legs to shift the energy around you before getting your day started or settling back into it.

Heart-Opening Meditation

............❋............

If you're feeling the need for love and peace, a nice heart-opening meditation could serve you well. Begin by setting your intention to open your heart to love and peace. You could say something like:

*As I sit in meditation, I focus on my heart's center
and fill it with love and harmony. So be it.*

Use whatever tools call to you. Maybe that's a nice-smelling incense you love, or you could spritz yourself and the area around you with some rose water, which is also good for your skin. Once your ambiance is set, you are ready to get into this heart-opening meditation.

As you begin, allow your eyes to close and start focusing on your heart's center. You can imagine colors of emerald green and/or hues of pink glowing from your chest, symbolizing the love you have to give to yourself and others. Invite that beautiful energy in and recognize that you are love. At the very basic level of our humanness, we are love, and if we walk through life with that energy, beautiful things can occur.

Imagine that light projecting forward from your heart's center until it is filling your space. Sit in that energy for as long as you'd like. Before opening your eyes, remind yourself that you are love, and your intention is to carry that feeling with you throughout your day wherever you go and with whomever you encounter.

Cord-Cutting Meditation

· · · · · · · · · · ❀ · · · · · · · · · ·

Many know this meditation as one that helps you cleanse from an ex. This is true. But it's so much more than that. When we engage in a cord-cutting meditation ritual, our intention is to sever energetic ties with someone else. This, of course, could be an ex-romantic partner, but it could also be an ex-friend, a toxic family member, or a combative coworker.

Cord-cutting rituals have existed for centuries with African and Indigenous roots. The ceremonies may be performed differently depending on the spiritual traditions practiced, but they serve the same purpose—to release a person or persons from energetic ties to another.

The Yaqui Indians from Sonora, Mexico, have a cord-cutting ceremony called Lutu Pahko, which is an all-night ritual that takes place one year after someone's death to release the family and community from mourning.

Shamanic cord-cutting rituals are quite different. The person connects with their spirit animal to support them in changing the energy of a current relationship. This ritual doesn't cut the cords entirely, but instead shifts the energy from unhealthy and unbalanced to healthy and enriching to a person's life force.

Here's a cord-cutting ritual you can try if you want to move on once and for all from someone in your life.

- Write their name down on a piece of paper.
- Light an orange candle to symbolize the sacral chakra, our energy center for creativity and our identity. Ask an adult to assist you and always use caution when working with open flames.
- As the candle burns, say words of release, like, "I release the energy of _____ from my aura."
- You can stare at the flame for an open-eyed meditation. It's amazing what the fire reveals when we stare into it long enough. Or you can close your eyes and visualize yourself physically cutting cords from that other person.
- If that's too difficult, make it more practical by getting some thread and cutting it with a scissor to symbolize your intention.
- Depending on the depth of your relationship, you may want to do this ritual more than once to really feel secure that you've cut the energetic ties and can move forward with a clean slate.
- Remember that you want to release them with love, even if they aren't the best person to be around. Send them away with love, which also enriches your soul and provides you with healing.
- Take the piece of paper and crush or tear it, placing it in a bowl of water before flushing it down the toilet or burying it in the dirt outside.

CHAPTER NINE

UNDERSTANDING THE CHAKRAS

We all have chakras, or energy centers, within our bodies that are tied to different things. Regardless of whether Indigenous spiritual wisdom called them chakras—a word that emerged in ancient Hindu philosophical texts called the Vedas—or not, the acknowledgment of these energy centers throughout our bodies is present. While there are many chakras throughout our bodies, we focus on seven major energy centers that are located along the spine from the base all the way up to the top of our heads. The chakras all have different meanings, are associated with various parts of the body and emotions, and are represented by colors and even sounds. These energy centers form a communication highway and can indicate the onset of disease and illness as well as feelings of being off-balance. The key to all of this work is balance, and the chakras are a great way to check in with yourself and pay special attention to the areas of your body, mind, and spirit that need it most. Let's get into it.

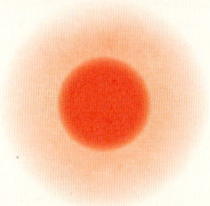

Root Chakra

············�֍············

The root chakra is our first energy center. It is located at the base of our spine, is represented by the color red, and is associated with the earth element. This is the area that is associated with us feeling safe and grounded in our lives. If you feel like you can't stand up for yourself or are constantly feeling guilty, it could be an indicator that your root chakra is off-balance.

Each chakra is associated with a sound or chant, and for the root it's *LAM*. Sit in meditation and breathe deeply. As you exhale, chant *LAM* and feel the vibration in your root chakra. This helps to balance that energy center and release you from feelings of fear and guilt.

You can also light a red candle to symbolize the need to show your root chakra some love, or you could buy yourself red flowers, and every time you see them smile and remind yourself that you're safe and don't need to worry. Eating red fruits and other foods can also stimulate the root chakra for balance. You can also get gemstones like ruby, red jasper, or fire agate and hold them as you meditate, place them by your bedside, or carry them with you throughout the day. The connections between colors, sounds, and our chakras are quite amazing, so have fun with them.

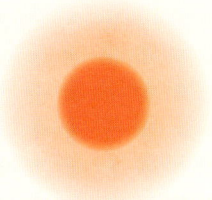

Sacral Chakra

* * * * * * * * * * * ✳ * * * * * * * * * * *

The sacral chakra is our second chakra. It is located approximately two inches below our belly button, is represented by the color orange, and is associated with the element of water. This is our center for creativity and sexuality. It's the womb center and the area of our sexual organs. Here is where our identity lives along with the beautiful things we want to create. Feelings of being stuck creatively may indicate the sacral chakra is off-balance.

You can restore balance by meditating similarly to what was discussed with the root chakra, except the chant would be *VAM* for this one. Or you can get up and move! The sacral chakra is like the waves of the ocean. So if you're feeling stagnant, moving your body will shift the energy within and around you. Dance, do yoga, go for a walk in nature, or go out and play. Gemstones that work well when balancing the sacral chakra are amber, orange tourmaline, and sunstone.

Solar Plexus Chakra

* * * * * * * * * * ✳ * * * * * * * * * *

The solar plexus chakra is the third energy center. It is located two inches above the belly button, is represented by the color yellow, and is associated with the element of fire. This is the center for self-worth, self-esteem, self-respect, and the ability to make decisions. If you are feeling self-conscious or harbor a lot of self-doubt, it is an indicator that the solar plexus chakra is off-balance.

To meditate and chant, use *RAM* for this chakra. Like with the other two, say *RAM* on the exhale. So deeply inhale, and on the exhale say, "Raaaaammmmm." Feel the vibration of the chant in the solar plexus chakra. This helps to bring balance to that energy center. You could also place both hands, one over the other, on the chakra and envision beautiful sun rays shining brightly through you and out into the room you're in. Imagine those rays filling the space and engulfing you in this beautifully warm, healing light from the sun. Go-to gemstones for solar plexus healing are yellow citrine, yellow tiger's eye, and yellow topaz, to name a few.

Heart Chakra

........·❋·...........

The heart chakra acts as the bridge for the chakras with the first three—the root, sacral, and solar plexus—representing our physical world, and the last three—the throat, third eye, and crown—representing our spiritual world. The heart is at the center of it all. Love is so powerful it can cure the world of its most toxic traits. If enough of us lived through love, our planet and human life would be healthier and happier because of it. So tending to the heart chakra is important.

It is located at the center of the chest, is represented by the color green, and is associated with the element of air. This is our center for love, compassion, and forgiveness. If you're experiencing heartache or grief in any way, the heart chakra is off-balance and needs some healing.

The heart-opening meditation from the last chapter would be great to assist with restoring balance to the heart chakra. Singing, praying, chanting YAM, and decluttering your space can also help bring back feelings of joy, tranquility, and peace to the heart center. Spritzing yourself with rose water is a great way to elevate feelings of love and compassion, therefore balancing the heart chakra. Gemstones for heart chakra balance include rose quartz, green tourmaline, peridot, and jade.

Throat Chakra

·············❋············

The throat chakra is our fifth chakra. It is located at the center of our throat, is represented by the color blue, and is associated with sound. It's not your typical element, but one could argue that it falls in the wind category since Indigenous spiritual wisdom associated music with wind.

This is a great chakra for chanting since it's connected to sound. Chant *HAM* and focus on the vibration in the throat. This is our center for expressing ourselves and knowing that our voice matters. If you are constantly being silenced, you have difficulty expressing yourself, or you hold back from displaying your creative talents, these are indicators that the throat chakra is off-balance. Chanting, singing, and praying out loud are wonderful ways to balance this energy center. Crystals like aquamarine, sodalite, turquoise, and blue kyanite work well to balance the throat.

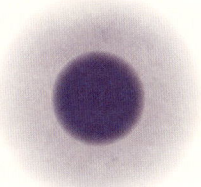

Third Eye Chakra

......................✳......................

The third eye chakra is our sixth chakra and is located between our eyebrows. This is the eye that can see far beyond our two eyes. It is associated with the color indigo and represents light. Imagine pulling a dark curtain back to see the sun. That's what you're essentially doing when working to balance the third eye chakra and keep it healthy. This is where your intuition thrives. Tapping into the third eye can help us see the bigger picture of our lives. It is our truth and our ability to learn from the experiences we go through in life.

If you have trouble trusting others, yourself, and situations, this indicates the third eye is off-balance. Chanting *OM* and focusing that energy in the third eye can help to restore balance. Visualization meditation is also great for third eye chakra balance. As you sit in meditation with your eyes closed, tap into that third eye. You can even massage it a little to jump-start the energy. Imagine seeing yourself in your most ideal form, living your best life. Everything has fallen into place, and your deepest desires have manifested. Watch yourself in this state for a while. When you feel ready, face yourself and ask, "How did you get here?" Then listen. You may be surprised by what you hear. Trust what comes up and thank yourself. This exercise reminds you that even though we often seek guidance externally, the answers are usually within us, and if we turn inward we can find them. Grab yourself a lapis lazuli, amethyst, or clear quartz crystal to amplify your healing for this energy center.

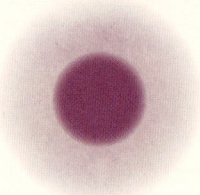

Crown Chakra

············ ✳ ············

The crown chakra is our seventh chakra and is located at the top, center of our head. This energy center is associated with three colors—purple, white, and gold—and as you meditate, you can summon the colors and trust in whichever one presents itself first. You may see all three!

The crown chakra is associated with thought and our connection to the Divine. If you are questioning your ability to trust life or your faith, this could indicate the crown chakra is off-balance. Chanting *AH* can help to open this center and balance it. Imagine that beautiful color that presented itself to you during meditation, and picture it as a glowing light flowing from the top of your head into the ether. This is your stairway to Source. Your connection to the Higher Power. Beyond the connection, it is also about trusting that even through your darkest days, there is something greater than yourself guiding and protecting you along your path.

Several crystals coincide with this chakra. Go-tos include amethyst, selenite, moonstone, and clear quartz.

CHAKRAS AT A GLANCE

CHAKRA	COLOR	SOUND	CRYSTAL
Root Chakra	Red	LAM	Red Jasper, Carnelian, Black Tourmaline, Bloodstone, Fire Quartz, Obsidian
Sacral Chakra	Orange	VAM	Tiger's Eye (orange), Orange Calcite, Carnelian, Sunstone, Amber
Solar Plexus Chakra	Yellow	RAM	Tiger's Eye (yellow), Lemon Quartz, Citrine, Pyrite, Yellow Topaz, Yellow Tourmaline
Heart Chakra	Green	YAM	Rose Quartz, Green Jade, Malachite, Green Aventurine, Emerald, Moss Agate, Peridot
Throat Chakra	Blue	HAM	Aquamarine, Lapis Lazuli, Blue Lace Agate, Turquoise, Amazonite
Third Eye Chakra	Indigo	OM	Amethyst, Fluorite, Sodalite, Clear Quartz, Kunzite, Obsidian
Crown Chakra	Gold, Purple, White	AH	Clear Quartz, Selenite, Howlite, White Agate, Fluorite, Amethyst, Angelite

CHAPTER TEN
LIMPIAS AND BAÑOS

The use of limpias, or spiritual cleansings, and baños, or herbal baths, has been a prominent part of Indigenous spiritual rituals for hundreds of years across Latin America. While the approach may be slightly different, the general intention of these spiritual rituals is the same—cleansing and revitalizing one's body, mind, emotions, and the aura of negative and stagnant energy.

The terms limpias and baños are often used interchangeably, but there is a difference. Water limpias use liquids like water, coconut milk, and Florida Water combined with herbs, flowers, and sometimes essential oils as they are poured over your body. Baños have similar ingredients, but you soak in them, setting intentions for energetic blockages to be removed from your body and carried down the drain with the spiritual bath.

Limpias can also be done using smoke, fire, and herbs. Smoke limpias can be carried out by burning sage or another sacred herb and allowing the smoke to float around your body or a space you want to spiritually cleanse. It can also be facilitated by a spiritual practitioner, curandera, bruja, or spiritualist—whatever they desire to be called. The facilitator will inhale deeply and exhale the sacred smoke around the person being cleansed. There may be prayer, chanting, singing, or meditation included as well.

Fire Limpias

· · · · · · · · · · · · ❋ · · · · · · · · · · · ·

Fire limpias are used as a gateway to the supernatural world. Ceremonies involving fire were among the most commonly practiced limpias in ancient Mesoamerica. These limpias were not only reserved for people but could also involve places, and it was believed they held the power to activate and renew the essence of a space. Yes—different physical spaces hold energy as well. So the next time you're home and feeling super cozy, look around at your space and say thanks. The energy will appreciate it and reciprocate with more good vibes.

Fire limpias can also shift streaks of bad luck, and burning a fire before beginning a spiritual ceremony or ritual can symbolize offering a fresh start.

Experienced curanderxs do white fire limpias, which are prepared and often combined with other spiritual works like pláticas, or heart-centered talks, as well as Spirit messages and soul-journeying meditation. The fire itself is carefully prepared in a big pot or cauldron using Epsom salt, rubbing alcohol, and dried herbs. They add a splash of alcohol to create a fire when a match is thrown into the pot. Traditionally, after the fire is going, the curanderx may add offerings like copal resin (to invite ancestors to the ritual), palo santo, and more herbs.

For you, a candle will do. The fire will symbolize the same. As the fire burns, it is cleansing the space and the person or persons it is intended for. Playing music is a great way to meditate on the fire as it burns and shifts the energy, removing blockages and bad juju, which is a word that originated in West Africa and describes bad luck or negative energy. In shamanic practices it is believed that there is good juju, which is protective and energizing, and bad juju, which can bring you down.

Egg Limpias

Egg limpias are also powerful ways to cleanse the aura, remove mal de ojo, and cleanse negative energy. The egg is believed to soak up all the icky stuff hanging around your energy and free you from it.

1. After setting your intention and giving gratitude for the egg and any other tools being used, you can clean the egg with a little Florida Water, light a candle (use caution and ask for an adult's help), and then the limpia de huevo (egg limpia) can begin.

2. The raw egg is passed over the body from head to toe either by oneself or a facilitator.

3. Afterward, the egg can be cracked into a clear glass of cold water with salt. You can also use Florida Water.

4. Watch as the egg sinks to the bottom of the glass and leave it alone for five minutes before reading it. Some believe that leaving it in longer will produce more results, but try not to go past ten minutes. That will be long enough.

5. The cup should not be moved or touched by you or anyone else. Let it do its thing before attempting to read the results of the egg limpia.

6. This last step is optional. Remember that you're setting your intention at the beginning of the ritual, so if you intend to use the egg to cleanse your aura and believe that it did, there's no need to read results. However, if you're interested in seeing what the egg picked up on, then reading it will be helpful.

READING YOUR EGG LIMPIA

When you look at your egg in the glass of water, remember not to move it; just look and observe what you see. You can even take a photo of it if you want to get a closer look. Whatever you see in the cup can explain why you've been feeling a certain way. The fact that it's in the cup is a good indicator that the egg has removed it from you.

○ Bubbles can symbolize the outcome of a successful limpia. If the bubbles are big, it may indicate others are talking about you.

○ Cloudiness may be present and could indicate the presence of physical ailments and mental fatigue. The limpia may have removed some, but it's a good idea to continue the healing with more limpias or other forms of spiritual cleansing. Wait a few days and do another egg limpia to see if it is clear or if the issue is still present.

- Strings show that you have an energetic connection with someone, and if this isn't something you want, a good cord-cutting ceremony could do the job of removing that energy from yours.
- Spikes relate to energetic blockages and gossip. Again, the egg may not have removed the blockages but instead is simply informing you that it's there and needs some attention and maintenance.
- If you see the shape of an eye on the center of the yolk, it is associated with mal de ojo, and you should work with a professional bruja or curandera to remedy the situation.
- You may also see a figure or figures in your egg yolk, which could indicate that energy vampires or bullies are present in your circle.

After the egg limpia is complete, it must be discarded safely by flushing it down the toilet, dumping it down the drain, or pouring it outside somewhere away from your home. It is not for consumption. Place the glass with other divination tools, and do not use it outside of spiritual work. This can be your egg limpia glass and nothing else.

Herbal Limpia

⁕

Herbal limpias, or barridas, are a way to cleanse the aura by sweeping herbs and/or flowers over a person's body. You can gather the herbs and flowers you'd like to use, tie them together in a bundle, spritz them with some Florida Water, and use a sweeping motion from head to toe, repeating it several times. Afterward, you can seal the limpia by using blessed water or an essential oil you intuitively connect with. Rub a little on the crown, third eye, throat, and heart chakras. Sealing the limpia means you are completing the ritual and sending your love and blessings for it to do its intended work.

If you want to elongate the cleansing, you can do this by splitting up your herbal or floral bundle between three paper plates and covering them with sea salt. Place the three plates under the bed at the head, chest or midsection, and feet. In curanderismo, it is believed that the cleansing will continue as you sleep and until the flowers and herbs have dried out. Once they're dry, you can discard them by burying them in the earth outside and away from your home or by throwing them in the garbage outside of your home.

New Moon Baño

........................❋........................

As we discussed earlier, new moons are a great time for manifesting things in your life.

Here's a simple way to create a new moon baño for a foot soak to attract abundance.

INGREDIENTS

1 green or red candle

2 to 3 tablespoons Florida Water

1 to 2 cups sea salt or Epsom salt

¼ cup each basil, cinnamon, and rosemary

½ to 1 cup orchid or peony petals

RITUAL

1. Light your green or red candle. The flame symbolizes the energetic cleanse you desire around your space and yourself and serves to prepare the area for your new moon baño. Remember to always use caution when working with open flames and ask an adult for help.

2. Fill a small bucket big enough for your feet with warm water and add the Florida Water, mixing it in with your hands.

3. Add the sea salt or Epsom salt and mix in with your hands until fully dissolved. Thank the water, the flame, and the salt for coming together to symbolize your intentions and magic.

4. Add the basil, cinnamon, and rosemary and mix in with your hands. Thank the herbs for their power. Your words ignite their magic.

5. Cover the top of your new moon baño with the flower petals. Orchids and peonies have been associated with wealth and prosperity throughout history.

6. Finally, say your wishes and intentions out loud. Everything you are calling in under the new moon can be spoken into the beautiful spiritual baño you created. Remember that water has memory, and your words create a beautiful tapestry of what you want within it.

7. Soak your feet in your new moon baño for 20 to 40 minutes. The first half of the baño will cleanse and heal you, and the second half will create the space needed to welcome in the new things.

The bottoms of our feet have thousands of energy points. Imagine the energy from the baño traveling up from the bottoms of your feet to your crown chakra, cleansing and healing you along the way.

Full Moon Limpia

·············❋·············

Here's one great way to get started with a full moon limpia. These easy-to-follow steps can help you raise your energetic vibration, so this is a great ritual to do if you're feeling more tired than usual or bored, sad, or angry. This energy reboot will help free your spirit from feeling dragged down, which could be the result of things happening in your own life or energy you've picked up from others around you. Whichever it is, and it can be a combination of both, this is why consistent limpias are great for spiritual maintenance.

1 candle (any color)

½ cup each chamomile and/or lavender

1 cup fresh rose petals

2 to 3 tablespoons Florida Water

2 to 3 tablespoons rose water (optional)

½ cup coconut milk

1 cup coconut water (optional)

RITUAL

1. Place all your ingredients on a countertop or table. Light the candle. The flame symbolizes the energetic cleanse you desire around your space and yourself to prepare the area for your full moon baño. Thank the flame for its cleansing properties, and thank all the ingredients you're bringing together to create magic. Please always use caution when working with open flames and ask for an adult's help.

2. Allow yourself to sit by the flame. Say thank you as you do this to acknowledge the powerful elements aligning. A great alternative to smoke is Florida Water, which will also cleanse the space, yourself, and your spiritual tools.

3. Bring some water to a gentle boil. Allow the water to cool to lukewarm for at least 10 minutes. Pour the water over a strainer filled with 1/2 cup of each herb you're using.

4. As the water falls into the bowl, continue praying, setting your intentions, speaking affirmations, singing, and giving thanks.

5. Add the Florida Water and the rose water, if using. Gently mix with your hands or a wooden spoon.

6. Add the coconut milk and mix it in with your hands. Then add the coconut water, if using. Coconuts are a symbol of happiness.

7. Cover the top of your limpia bowl with the remaining fresh rose petals. If you can, try to get organic ones, but if not, regular store-bought petals are just fine as long as you clean them to remove pesticides. You can do this by soaking the petals in a mix of 2 cups of cold water, 2 tablespoons of lemon juice, and 4 tablespoons of baking soda. Soak the petals for 20 minutes or more and rinse several times with water. Roses carry the highest frequency of love. So give yourself the ultimate self-love gift with this renewing limpia.

8. Gently place your hands or your feet into the limpia. Think of your intention and feel the magic flow up your arms or feet and throughout the rest of your body as you immerse your hands or feet.

9. Don't rinse off. Just air-dry if you can or pat dry with a light-colored towel.

10. Journal, meditate, go for a walk, dance, or do whatever you feel called to do. If you're feeling like you need a nap, honor your body.

Remember that with this easy-to-follow limpia, you are incorporating all the elements. Fire and air are represented in the flame. The water element is honored in the boiled water, Florida Water, coconut water, and rose water, and earth is represented with the herbs and flowers.

An alternative would be to make the limpia, pour it into a spray bottle, and spritz it over your crown and all around you. You can even use it to lightly spray your bed and pillows before going to bed.

CHAPTER ELEVEN
MORE TOOLS FOR INSIGHT

Tarot

Although tarot did not originate in Latin America, it is a useful tool for guidance and wisdom about your life and the path you've already traveled, where you are today, and what may be next in your evolution. Today, many brujas use tarot as a go-to divination tool that works on its own or paired with other tools, depending on the ritual.

The first tarot decks showed up in the early fifteenth century in Northern Italy, and tarot was considered a card game, not a spiritual practice or tool. As this card game traveled to Southern France, it started to take on a new meaning with mystical interpretations. The French viewed the cards as revealing information about ourselves, others around us, and our lives. The Marseilles deck was the first deck used, followed by the widely known Rider-Waite-Smith deck. A woman named Pamela Colman Smith was the artist who designed the Rider-Waite-Smith deck, a huge feat for a female artist in the early twentieth century.

Today, tarot is used in many spiritual practices around the world. It includes seventy-eight cards, of which twenty-two are called major arcana, and fifty-six are called minor arcana. The major arcana are associated with the human journey and include cards like Strength, The Empress, The Magician, The Sun, and The Moon.

The minor arcana cards zoom in on a current situation you may be facing in your life. They include four suits—wands, cups, swords, and coins or pentacles—and each suit is numbered between two and ten and includes an ace and four court cards: King, Queen, Knight, and Page. Each suit is associated with an element and a specific area of life. Wands are symbolic of ideas and jobs and are associated with the element of fire. Cups are the emotional suit, representing the water element. Swords are associated with masculinity, intellect, sorrow, misfortune, and the element of air. Coins or pentacles represent the earth element, the physical body, and wealth or abundance.

When you buy a new deck, familiarize yourself with it. Connect to the cards by looking at each one and then shuffling and seeing which cards come out. You can pull one card for yourself every morning to help guide you through that day, or you might draw a card whenever you feel called to do so. Card readings are often associated with the moon cycles—eight different phases occurring approximately every 29.5 days—which include the new and full moon as well as the waxing crescent, first quarter, waxing gibbous, waning gibbous, third quarter, and waning crescent. The major moon cycles that tarot readings are often associated with are the new and full moon. Tarot card readings are also big with topics like love, work, family, and predictions of the future, among many other interpretations.

Here's one you can try if you're just starting out with tarot.

1. Shuffle the deck and as you do so, say a little prayer or set an intention.

2. If any cards fall out while you're shuffling, set them aside.

3. When you feel intuitively ready to stop shuffling, pull three cards—representing past, present, and future—from left to right.

4. Read the cards like a story, and see the meaning of them by referring to the book included with your deck, if it has one, or by simply feeling what the cards are saying to you.

At first it will feel like learning a new language. Keep going. It will become second nature if you do, and you will soon be able to do the readings without the help of the booklet.

Oracle Cards

Oracle cards are a great complement to tarot cards, but they can also be used alone in readings. The biggest difference is that oracle cards aren't categorized like the tarot, which includes major and minor arcana cards and various suits. Oracle cards may have deck themes like angels and ancestors or even fairies.

Like tarot cards, oracle cards often come with a booklet that defines what each card means. It's a good idea to familiarize yourself with the deck you choose to take home. Look at each card and see how it makes you feel. Maybe you can try to intuitively grasp its meaning. Then read the book to see if you're on point or need a bit more direction on what it means.

Oracle cards are great for self-reflection and exploring what you've been feeling on a deeper level. Sometimes it feels like the Universe is trying to communicate with us, and oracle cards are a great option for gaining clarity on what those messages are and how you can utilize this information.

Astrology

Astrology shows how the moon, sun, planets, stars, and other celestial bodies or matter in the Universe were positioned at the time of your birth, and how that translates into all the characteristics that make you who you are. It is believed that astrology can interpret how the positions of these celestial bodies influence our lives here on planet Earth.

Just like people check the weather forecast daily to see whether they should wear a jacket or carry an umbrella, checking the astrological transits is also important for daily life. The astrology forecast can offer direction and guidance on what's going on with the sun, moon, stars, and planets and how that will impact our personal lives.

During eclipse season, which occurs at various times during the year and includes a lunar eclipse and solar eclipse taking place in close proximity to each other, the energy is considered quite powerful and transformative. It's a time when introspection is important to discern where change needs to occur in your life.

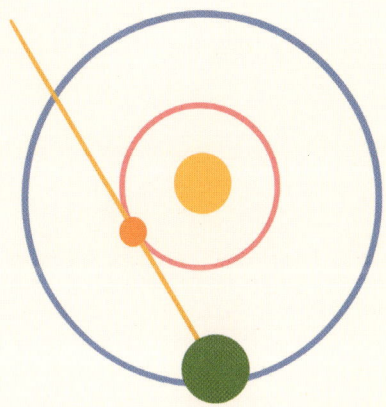

Mercury retrograde is an astrological transit that occurs three to four times a year and is often a hot topic on social media and in pop culture. During this time, Mercury's rotation slows so much that it appears to be moving backward. It's an optical illusion, but this seemingly backward movement is believed to impact a variety of things in our daily lives like technology, communication, and travel. It's highly recommended during this time to back up computers, hold off on making travel arrangements or going on trips, and pay close attention to how you are communicating with yourself and others. Mercury isn't the only planet to go into retrograde. All the planets are impacted by this at some point, but Mercury retrograde seems to be the one everyone wants to know about the most.

Instruments

........·✻·........

Instruments like rattles, maracas, and a variety of drums, horns, sound bowls, and flutes have been used for generations in Indigenous spiritual practices. Remember that the sounds they deliver are represented by the water and air elements, so it makes sense that these divination tools help to elevate spiritual practices and rituals.

Rattles have been used in many spiritual traditions to clear and shift energy and summon our ancestors. The maraca, which is a hand percussion instrument usually played in pairs, is used in a similar fashion.

Drums are an important part of many Indigenous spiritual practices, rituals, and celebrations. From congas to batá, a double-headed hourglass drum played on both sides that is used in spiritual rituals and public festivals, drums hold a special place in Indigenous life. The Taínos used the mayohuacán, which was a wooden slit drum played during sacred ceremonies called areytos.

Horns are used throughout spiritual rituals and ceremonies. One way is by blowing a horn once in each of the four directions to honor the balance of life at the beginning of a ritual. They're also used to end a ceremony by showing gratitude for the elements and our ancestors who assisted in the ritual. During a ceremony, drums may be used to invoke or invite ancestors and deities.

Sound bowls are a divination tool used in many different spiritual practices. The way the sound vibrates from the bowls can ease anxiety and tension, help the flow of blocked energy, and create feelings of peace and relaxation. Similarly, the sound of a flute can help improve energy flow and invoke a spiritual awakening. The flute's song can carry you through meditation as your soul journeys to different spaces and time.

Pendulum

············❋············

Pendulums are used to help locate areas of the body where energy is blocked or off-balance. A pendulum is a great tool to use with energy-healing practices like Reiki, which works to align the chakras and ease stress and anxiety. Holding the pendulum over your open palm or the area of the body you're working on will show you if the energy is flowing nicely or if it may be blocked. If the pendulum creates a clockwise rotation, it symbolizes good energy flow. If it doesn't swing at all or barely moves, that's an indication of stagnant or stuck energy. If it rotates counterclockwise, it can indicate the presence of negative energy or mal de ojo. Once the area that needs some extra love is identified, you can focus on healing and balancing those energy centers to help cleanse the mind and body and gain clarity.

Journaling

.... ❋ ....

One divination tool that's quite powerful is journaling. You can create a gratitude journal to record daily thoughts about the things you are thankful for in your life, which invites feelings of joy and peace. Journaling can also help declutter the mind. When you're overwhelmed or confused, try writing down your thoughts. Release everything you're feeling on those pages. Don't worry about penmanship, grammar, or punctuation. Just write. You'll be amazed at how much you've energetically let go of just by unpacking your thoughts on the page.

CHAPTER TWELVE
PRACTICAL MAGIC IN DAILY LIFE

We've covered a wide variety of rituals and practices you can incorporate for your own spiritual wellness. Now it's time to put them to use in your everyday life. Remember that being a bruja, a curandera, a spiritualist, or a mystic is a lifestyle choice, not a Band-Aid solution to life's problems. Healing from past traumas is an ongoing practice. It's likely that one ritual or ceremony won't heal you completely. Over time, when we adopt these practices into our lives, they can heal us, release negativity, and prepare us to better face and heal from future obstacles.

Remember that the spiritual practices outlined in this book are a great complement to a regular health routine, like annual physicals and mental health therapy. Always talk to an adult or professional if you are experiencing mental or physical health issues and need help.

Morning Practices

············❋············

In the morning, consider including a gratitude practice where you simply say thanks for all the things in your life, big and small. It can be a simple acknowledgment that you have toothpaste and a toothbrush for dental care and a shower and soap to clean your body, face, and hair. Your gratitude may also be something that's an even bigger life moment like graduating from high school and getting into the college of your choice. Or maybe you're grateful for how much you've grown through your healing journey. That is definitely something to be grateful for.

Other great morning spiritual rituals you could easily incorporate into your life are pulling a card for the day, meditation, stretching or some form of movement, and spiritual protection. If you do nothing else, remember to protect your energy before leaving the house. You can spritz some Florida Water on yourself or imagine a beautiful light forming around you, protecting you from other people's energy and exterior forces that you do not want to bring back home with you.

Do your very best to not look at your phone for at least the first thirty minutes to an hour after you wake up. Instead, replace the morning social media scrolling with spoken affirmations. This will positively impact your mindset and energy far more than social media can.

Evening Practices

＊

One great way to wrap up your day and ensure you are falling asleep feeling good is by having a gratitude rock or stone by your bedside. Before you fall asleep, hold it in your hand and think about one good thing that happened that day. Even on the most challenging days there is something good that happens. You may have to dig a little deeper, but it's there, even if the best part of your day is lying in bed holding your gratitude rock. And if that's the case, say it. Whatever you choose, just acknowledge it by thinking about it silently or saying it out loud. It may bring a smile to your face. What a great way to go to bed!

Journaling at night is another great evening practice. Let the day go on the page and release it from your energy. Once it's on the page, close the book. You don't ever have to read it again unless you want to. A great alternative to writing in a journal is recording voice notes. You can allow yourself to say everything that's on your mind and in your heart. Then end the recording, and if you want to revisit it again in the future, it's there. If not, you don't ever have to listen to it again. The release is healing enough.

Protect Your Energy

⋯⋯⋯⋯⋯✳⋯⋯⋯⋯⋯

Protecting your energy is important and was mentioned above. Here, we dig a little deeper into why it's so important. Our aura is an electro-magnetic field that surrounds our body in an oval shape. This field can stretch outward for several feet and may therefore collide with other people's energy. When we protect our energy, we are ensuring that we don't absorb anyone else's energy or give ours away.

Envisioning a light around you protecting your aura is one great way, as is spraying yourself with Florida Water with the intention of using it for spiritual protection. You could also carry a crystal with you that is good for spiritual protection like black tourmaline or selenite. Keep it in your pocket throughout the day, and if you ever experience a moment when you need some spiritual protection, simply touch the crystal and remind yourself that you are safe.

You can also keep a small spray bottle of Florida Water with you, and whenever you feel the need to refresh your spiritual protection, you can spray some on your hands and inhale deeply, imagining that this revives that energy bubble you placed around yourself in the morning.

Protect Your Space

·········❋··········

As mentioned previously, our bedrooms, other spaces in our home, and our spaces in school carry energy, and when we show gratitude, it reciprocates. You can show the love you have for your bedroom by cleansing your space consistently. Remember to always be cautious when using fire and ask for an adult's help. Whether you use sage, palo santo, a candle, or you sing, dance, and incorporate music or sound to uplift the energy of your room, it doesn't matter. The intention to spiritually cleanse your personal space is what is important.

Opening the windows and doors to allow air to circulate through your personal space is a great way to eliminate stagnant energy. Placing bowls of water on high surfaces like the top of your dresser or a bookshelf can help to soak up negative energy and keep your bedroom feeling energetically fresh. Change the water weekly or monthly to make sure that spiritual maintenance is intact. Remember that your intention is everything. The tools you use are a complement to the intentions you set at the beginning of any spiritual ritual.

How to Pray

·········❋··········

One of the biggest lessons in this book is to listen to your intuition, that inner voice helping to guide you in life. This pertains to praying as well. There is no one way to pray. Some people get on their knees to pray, some pray by singing, and others may incorporate dancing into their prayers. This is your way of conversing with the Higher Power. So don't overthink it.

If you've never done it before, you can start by putting your hands in prayer position, palms against each other with your fingers pointing up and your closed hands close to your heart. Then tap into what you need to say. The words may not come out right away, but give it a moment and it may surprise you what eventually does come. Speak to God and share whatever it is you want to say or ask for. You can pray for yourself, another person, a group of people, or the collective of everyone and everything in the Universe. There are no rules. Your relationship with the Higher Power is very much your own. So make it what you will. Remind yourself that you are never alone. Even on the days when you feel lonely, you can talk to Spirit.

Here's an example of a prayer for someone who may be finding it difficult to make a choice about something important in their life:

Great Spirit, I pray that you guide me through this decision-
making process. I feel lost, and I don't know what to do.
Please give me a sign or help me to see the path that is mine.
I know I am safe to move forward with your guidance
and protection and the support of my spirit team.
Thank you for your presence in my life
and the lives of those I love. So be it.

After you're done praying, you may want to sit in stillness for a moment and see if any messages come up. If not, close your prayer in any way that feels right to you. "So be it" is a closing phrase used in many Indigenous practices and may have some slight variations. I say, "Han Han Katú. Han Han Katú," which means "So be it" in Taíno and has different spellings. At times, I feel called to say "Amen." Again, make it your own and do what feels right to you.

On Healing
Through the Work

❊

Healing will allow you to shine your light unapologetically as you live through love and kindness, and it will give you the ability to navigate life during the good and the not-so-good times. Life is a journey—one that can be beautiful beyond our greatest imaginations. We're responsible for acknowledging our connection to everything and everyone around us, living life with kindness in our hearts, and working through shadows for continued personal growth. When things aren't going our way, this may be a challenging way to be, but rest assured that no matter what darkness we may face in our lives, that beautiful life force energy—that light, our light—still shines. Creating healthy boundaries in your life will help to keep you feeling safe. Don't ever dim your light for another. Shine your light brightly and be a part of healing the world simply by healing yourself and living in your truth.

The Latine experience in the United States comes with its own unique challenges, including parents who have immigrated from another country, or if you moved to the States when you were younger and didn't speak the language. Remember the tools outlined in this book—they are for you. Your light is still beautifully bright even if you've faced more challenges in life than the average young person your age. The circumstances we are born into do not change our ability to heal and shine brightly.

Performing Rituals on Other People and Pets

As you deepen your spiritual practices and understanding of what being bruja means, always begin with yourself first. Once you feel more confident working your magic, you can offer to perform rituals and spiritual practices on other people and your animal companions as well.

Working with people you're close to is a great way to continue learning and deepening your practice. Not everyone will be open to it, so seek out those who are willing to give it a try and have an open mind about it.

Whether it's doing a tarot reading for someone else or performing an egg limpia on them, take your time and use your intuition to help guide you to how they're feeling and what they need. As you continue these offerings, you'll become more comfortable and knowledgeable with your magic.

Be gentle with the person you're working with, and it's a good idea to explain each step as you go or at the beginning of the ritual. Let the person know what you're going to be doing and what they can expect. For example, if you begin your ritual by using Florida Water to cleanse them, be sure to explain that you're spraying it in their hands or around them to cleanse their energy and prepare them for the ritual. Then move on to the next steps. This will help build trust between you and the person or animal you're working with.

CONCLUSION

How to Go Forth with Your Magic

·············✷·············

It's a beautiful journey when we embrace the magic within us and learn how to use it to better our lives, feel more aligned with our surroundings, and heal ourselves and others. Now that you've started your journey to better understand the light and shadows within yourself, you can begin to uncover so many things about life and the role you play in this human journey.

The best way to use this book is to pair it with your intuition. What really spoke to you and intrigued you to learn more? Maybe there are practices and rituals outlined that really resonate with you. If so, this could be a calling to go deeper and learn more about it. Where does that call show up in your physical body? Maybe it is in your shoulders or your stomach. Place your hands there and send yourself some love. Breathe deeply to calm down and regulate your system. This is what it means to be in communication with your body. Learning to communicate with your body and listening to your intuition are key to being bruja. Become the watcher of your body and mind, and your spirit will thank you.

You are the star of your life and deserve to be treated with the utmost respect and love. Don't ever forget it. The magic you bring into this world is a blessing, and if you are feeling the call to be your bruja self, go for it! The world needs your gifts.

ACKNOWLEDGMENTS

Spirit has guided me from the beginning of this book-writing process. I allowed the flow of creativity to work through me as I typed the words on the page. Others supported me throughout the process as well, even if they didn't know it. During the entire time I was writing this book, my Titi Carmen was battling cancer. Her lovely spirit shined through until the very end when she transitioned from this human life on June 4, 2024. The last time I saw her, I held her hand and sang softly in her ear. She was struggling to speak, but after I finished singing, she said, "I heard you." Now, she has joined my spirit team as a powerful ancestor. Titi Carmen was always so sweet to me and constantly cheered me on as a writer, a mother, and a woman. So, thank you, Titi Carmen, for being you. You will truly be missed in this human life, but I know your spirit lives on and is still present in the lives of those you love.

I also want to thank my mother, Rafaela Rivera, who has always supported me as a writer even when I was scribbling poetry in my journal at the age of nine. She always had the time to sit and listen to a new story, poem, or song I wrote, and still does today. I will be forever grateful for my mother and the resilient woman she is—pure magic. And thank you to my Bruja sisters, Kathy and Damaris, who I love so much, and to our matriarch, Mama.

Thank you to my high school English teacher, Mr. DePeter, who was the first one to inspire me to become a writer. I wrote a poem for my class when I graduated from New London High School in New London, Connecticut. Mr. DePeter read it and told me, "You could be a professional writer." I never heard those words spoken before and without him knowing, he planted the seed that would change the trajectory of my life forever. Good teachers can have a profound impact on a young person's life.

I want to also acknowledge the many spiritual teachers that have come into my life because their knowledge and care has brought me to a place of feeling confident in my magic. A special shout-out to Priscilla Colon, founder of Casa Areyto, for providing insight and knowledge to me during the process of writing this book. I am grateful for you, amiga.

Finally, to my three children, I thank all of you for being my muses. You are the spark to my flame, the beat to my heart, and the light of my life. I truly found my magic when you entered my life. First, with my eldest, who I shared eleven years with before welcoming my twins. I live and breathe in gratitude for the three of you, always.

ABOUT THE AUTHOR

For more than twenty years, Zayda Rivera has been writing for a variety of publications, covering everything from entertainment, breaking news, pop culture, politics, lifestyle, parenting, women's issues, spirituality, and astrology. She was a featured poet in a spoken word tour, has hosted events and moderated panel discussions many times over the course of her career, and is the executive producer for many high-profile award galas and community events.

Zayda lives in gratitude and helps others live a life of truth and presence through her business, Mindful Living with Z, which she launched in 2019 right before the pandemic. Her business grew through virtual sessions with people all around the country and internationally, who were looking for spiritual guidance and support during one of the most challenging times in recent history. Zayda is grateful every day that she listened to the deep inner-knowing which was telling her to study and learn how to work with energy as a Reiki Master, and with tarot, meditation, and yoga.

Her biggest achievements to date are her three lovely children. Zayda truly believes that we all are the cocreators of life with God, and when we walk in that knowledge every step of the way, life is magical and beautiful beyond anything we can imagine.

ABOUT THE ILLUSTRATOR

Jennifer Dahbura is an illustrator from El Salvador, Central America, and has been working as an illustrator since 2014. Growing up surrounded by strong women, her art reflects the deep influence of those relationships. Characterized by vibrant colors, rich textures, and intricate patterns, her work draws inspiration from Salvadoran culture and the natural world around her. Gathering the mysticism of the legends and traditions into a magical, mystical imprint in her art. Jennifer's illustrations combine folklore, human emotions, and the beauty of nature. She has worked on editorial, commercial, and branding projects, always incorporating her narrative style into each creation.